# ONE

## Perception

When I was a child my family took my grandmother to the mountains on a day trip. She had never been before and I remember that she was nervous as we approached our destination. Another thing I remember is her telling us how surprised she had been that the road went around in curves and not up and down with the lay of the hills. Her preconceived notion was not exactly reality and it changed her opinion of and desire to revisit with us again. I guess she enjoyed the trip. We all have preconceived notions about what we believe to be true, what we think about people we know and about what we think of people (or groups) whom we do not know. As a child we perceive time to move at much slower pace than it truly does even to the point of seeing a mature adult more elderly than they really are. The ripe old age of sixty looks entirely different when you are fifty-nine, than when you are a child of nine.

People who are close to me know that I am a Virginian through and through. People who do not know me as well may perceive me to be southern which would be true. The question is what is preconceived as a "southerner"? Is it drinking sweet tea, loving grits, fried chicken and cornbread? Or maybe it is speaking with a drawl, loving the simplicity of the country side, and going barefoot. Whatever is preconceived about being a southerner would most likely be what someone who does not know me would think. The truth is I do not like iced tea, but all the rest, fits me to a tee. So I am both Virginian and southern, and proud of it. (Disclaimer, there are many varied and amazing qualities to being southern, too many to list here and now.)

Another preconceived notion that some people have is that of being a Christian. Some people base their opinions on very little real knowledge, others, by what they see and hear from those that call themselves Christians. Speaking with someone not too long ago I realized what an impact our actions, our voices have with those who have a preconceived idea of what and who we are supposed to be as we go about in this world carrying our banner of the cross. We obviously are doing more harm than good when we visit church on Sunday but show up at the restaurant on Friday night with someone other than to whom we are married. Going to bible study on Wednesday night but caught stealing from the place of employment does not show Christians in either a good or true light. To reach a world with preconceived notions about what it means to be Christian we should approach with caution, watching our words and our actions.

I asked my husband what he thought of me (his preconceived idea) when he had first met me and how he felt now when he considered who I am. He answered easily saying, "You are full of life, a giver, a writer, mother and sister and most of all a Christian through and through. I was really pleased by his answer and yet I had to push him one step further. Asking him if he thought I was "southern" he grinned and replied, "My preconceived notion was this woman is country to the core, but I have come to know you and yes you are as southern as anyone else from Virginia." I have to admit though that I was really complimented by his perceived truth that I am a Christian...

# TWO

## They Are Only Nails

When I recently wanted to extend my husband's and mine giving to a new family of missionaries, my husband suggested that I may need to give up something that I spend that extra money on each month. So I did some "soul searching" praying that the Lord would convict me to know what in my life I was willing to sacrifice.

Unfortunately for my nail technician I decided to give up having my manicure every few weeks. She understood, graciously I may say, but my nails have suffered. As I was talking to a good friend one day I showed my hands to her and as we (I) despondently discussed my nail predicament, we claimed a truth for me, "They're only nails after all!"

This of course set my mind to thinking about all those things in my life that I may choose to label, "important", "can't live without", "got to have", but actually have little if no affect on any real part of my life. It serves to remind me of everything that I hold dear in my heart may also be things that I put before God. Let me rephrase, that I do put before God.

I feel that I am standing at a crossroads of my life. God must come first and the time is now that he is asking me to begin sacrificing the things that I have held dear or deemed necessary. Along with this change I must clearly recognize what other areas of my life I have need to weed through, clearing the rubbage that clearly gets in the way of my true purpose on this earth. As I look around at all the waste of time and money in my life I know that I can be a much more efficient steward of what God has given me.

"They're only nails after all", right? Strange how that one line brings me to the sacrifice that Jesus made on the cross. As he made his way to Calvary carrying a tree upon his back did he say to his Father in Heaven, "They're only nails after all?"

# THREE

# Awards

Man gives awards, God gives rewards. In light of controversial topic, which I will neither write about nor discuss, the idea came to me that "awards" are man's way of giving out a viable alternative to rewards. With the exception of the Nobel peace prize winners, most don't receive money along with the manmade award. God rewards His children for being faithful followers and good disciples. God's rewards cannot be pulled from some random list of "you did this, so I will give you that," and they are unique to each recipient. Hebrews 11:6 " And without faith it is impossible to please him, for whoever would draw near to God must believe that he exists and that he rewards those who seek him."

Jeremiah 17:10 "I the LORD search the heart and test the mind, to give every man according to his ways, according to the fruit of his deeds." God absolutely rewards us for the good and righteous things we do in His name and for His glory. He does not hand out awards for courage, artisanship or championship in life, yet as our Father who is proud of our accomplishments I believe that He is watching over our achievements. The rewards come when our achievements yield fruit. This is unlike anything else we receive in this life and carries on into our next. We work for man, we receive compensation in the form of a paycheck, we marry and begin a family, and God rewards us with a child. The best in sport wins a trophy, we run the race to live a good and honorable life in God's will and we are rewarded with eternal life. Revelation 22:12 "Behold, I am coming soon, bringing my recompense with me, to repay everyone for what he has done."

Being awarded the top prize is an amazing honor and something to be proud of, no matter what anyone else believes about who is more deserving or who worked harder to win. The honor though, is fleeting, as is the fame and attention it may bring with it. Being rewarded by our Father in Heaven is everlasting. We are given exactly what we deserve by His design and never man's and though this is difficult at times to understand we must trust that God always has a plan. We see the hungry, the homeless, the dying and ask, where then is their reward? I believe that God is calling each of us to be their reward; as we feed the hungry, shelter the homeless and comfort the dying. Galatians 6:9 "And let us not grow weary of doing good, for in due season we will reap, if we do not give up."

# FOUR

## Hopes and Dreams

I was thinking about my "hopes" and "dreams" and how they are different now that I have become a mature adult versus what they were when I was a younger. Strangely enough they have not changed that much at all; only how I go about achieving them has changed. When I was younger I wanted a family and home, a decent job and happiness. Now I seek happiness as well but I go about looking for it in a completely different way, through my spirit not my flesh. I look towards God and His will in my life through Jesus Christ to find any true happiness that any of those elements, family, home and career brings.

There is a definite distinction between my hope from years ago and my heart's desire today. I have discovered the value of happiness in the wonders of God's world around me. Growing in wisdom has simplified my desires and separated them from my needs. What I strived for in my youth can now be described as what I had to have to survive, things of the flesh: a roof over my head, food in my stomach, clothing and all the accessories that I thought I had to have. I have discovered that those things provided only an instance of true happiness, a fleeting moment of joy, joy that dissipated as quickly as it appeared. My hope has changed, my heart desires much more than a moment of pleasure, I need a lifetime of joy.

I am putting my hope and my faith in the saving grace of my God. I have come to understand and recognize the true steadfast happiness and lasting joy can come, not from things of the flesh but from the spirit. The long term gift of happiness, which is the essence of all that we struggle to achieve, can only be obtained and held onto through the Holy Spirit and His comfort, truths and love that, engulfs my soul. The world holds an illusion of happiness, a mere taste of joy that is gone as quickly as it appears. The spirit knows and responds to the river of everlasting life, love and happiness that sustains us through all the days of our lives.

Yes, my "hopes" and "dreams" have taken a drastic change throughout the years and for this I am eternally grateful. As well I am  completely optimistic that the things my spirit craves are so much more able to give me lasting happiness and joy then anything this world, which satisfies my flesh, could ever give to me. My hope is now that I can share with those who are still looking for happiness. That those who are still seeking to find their "hope" and "dreams", will see through my life and the joy of my spirit, that the only long lasting happiness lies in the knowledge of Jesus. Jesus as your guide, your savior, your hope; everlasting to everlasting, in this world and on into the fellowship of Jesus for eternity, that beloved is true happiness.

# FIVE

## Patterns

My parking has gotten very erratic; I cannot seem to get my vehicle between the white lines to save my life. Every place I pull into, whether there are other cars parked or an empty parking lot, I am off by several inches. Thank goodness I have yet to hit another car. Of course, like many things do, this makes me stop and consider what other signs show me that my life may be off by a few inches.

My sleeping pattern has gone off the charts; I am in bed by ten, asleep at eleven, awake at three, four, five...getting a good night's sleep some of the time and some time not much at all.

My reading habits have changed. I used to start a book and devour it in days, sometimes hours. These days I have three or four books going at once and it takes weeks if not months to finish one. What has not changed is that I love to read!

My emotional being is showing signs of deterioration as I cry at the drop of a hat, laugh uncontrollably at the weirdest stuff and yet I find joy in the most simple of things, actually more like when I was a child. Could this be part of what I have heard called a "second childhood"; if so the simplicity of childish joys is welcome here.

My eating behavior has changed dramatically. Off and on diets, craving chocolate one day and fresh vegetables the next; I cannot seem to get myself into a pattern that is sustainable. Recently I discussed with a friend that at my age I am getting tired of the fuss over weight issues, so I believe that I am drawing the lines on diets. Do you think I can stay in between those lines?

Whether it is due to getting older or not, my husband says it is time I rethink how I drive and how quickly I pull into a parking spot. My struggle may be with perception, it could be my eyesight, or it could be that I seem to be always in a thousand hurries. Whatever the reason, I believe that I need to focus on all these little things that are throwing me off an inch or so in my daily life; it is only a matter of time before I entirely misjudge that parking spot and ram into another vehicle.

# SIX
## Measures

We measure everything, weight, height, money, intelligence, wealth and power. We weigh bodies and when we are not so happy with the number we start measuring the amount of food we put into our mouths. We measure our children as they grow keeping records in baby books and with marks on the door frames. We measure our intelligence by how well we do in school, tracking with grades, report cards and diplomas. We measure our financial wealth with bank account balances, purchases and debts. A nation is measured by its power which comes from its military, its financial standings, and its population, among other factors. We measure love. Yes, we take a look at each other, our families, our church, our spouses and we measure that love based entirely upon relationship.

A love we cannot measure is God's love for us, His children, His creation, His world. Psalm 103:11-12 "For as high as the heavens are above the earth, so great is his steadfast love toward those who fear him; as far as the east is from the west, so far does he remove our transgressions from us." What better measurement of love can there be than this, without measure, endless, steadfast and completely without fear of repercussions as long as we understand and love Him with our entire being. God's love has no measure.

God is able to measure our love for Him through our relationship with Jesus Christ. Mark 12:30 "And you shall love the Lord your God with all your heart and with all your soul and with all your mind and with all your strength." We have a measure to show our love for Him, it is "all", everything we have, our hearts, souls and minds. Ephesians 6:24 "Grace be with all who love our Lord Jesus Christ with love incorruptible." This then is how to measure our love for Him, with love so strong, so deep, so committed that it is incorruptible.

We show others by what measure we love God through how we love them and keep His commandments. 1 John 5:3 "For this is the love of God, that we keep his commandments. And his commandments are not burdensome." Jesus says "Greater love has no one than this that someone lay down his life for his friends." I have never yet been called to this extreme but try with everything within me to express my love for my fellow man.

I enjoy writing and measure my success with the pleasure I hope I am giving to others. I also measure my joy in the hearts that are touched and I pray moved to agree with my ministry. So much of our lives are measured by the world's standards but I am happier measuring mine by God's grace, mercy and His steadfast love for me.

# SEVEN

## Memory Lane

Oh how I love walking down memory lane and on a recent work trip with my sister we did just that. We reminded each other of things that we had forgotten and told stories that we had never heard or at least had not remembered. One of my most cherished memories is visiting the library; I believe it was an oasis for a child who needed a refuge occasionally. What I did not remember was taking my sister, six years my junior, for her first visit to the place where dreams resided.

As we drove down the back roads of North Carolina reminiscing she told me of the time that I took her to my safe haven, my favorite place on earth, the library, to check out her own book, The Baby Duck or some such children's book. She remembers her big sister taking her by the hand, leading the way down the cracked and uneven sidewalks, patiently matching steps to make sure that they stayed in time. I was a good big sister. Actually I think I still am one. The conversation was sweet, refreshing and poignant as we shared a common love, books, with an event from our past. I was moved by the thought of leading my little sister to share my favorite place and my love for books. I may not share the actual memory with her, but share the love, yes indeed.

A trip down memory lane was just what was needed for my sister and me as we recalled precious moments long since forgotten, if known at all. The importance of our past can only be valued by keeping it alive through the sharing. I believe that is the one of the many reasons, and there are a lot, I love books as they not only store up facts and fiction, they help us keep for all time the cherished memories of our lives.

# EIGHT

## The Wilderness

I believe a time comes for each of us to go to into the wilderness, experiencing our own spiritual reawakening. We need space away from what is happening in the world for a while, spending time meditating and communing with God with no distractions. A fasting and praying wilderness where the Holy Spirit can fill us once again with renewed vigor and excitement for our life's ministry. Exploring the endless possibilities of what God would have us do to use the rest of our life for His glory, calls for an immeasurable time of soul searching for truth.

God is calling me into a time of wilderness. I have every hope and complete faith that He will revive my spirit and return me refreshed and cleansed. Psalms 107:35 "He turns a desert into pools of water, a parched land into springs of water." I know that this one woman's journey will experience a time of refreshing as God sees and understands my dryness as I thirst for clarity and honest testimony. A few days, weeks, whatever it may take wandering in my wilderness is what I feel led to do, so I must. I know that His desire for me is to not only find my own peace and happiness but to be spiritually healthy in order to continue the ministry that He has given to me.

Psalms 55:7 "Yes, I would wander far away; I would lodge in the wilderness; Selah " I too, as the psalmist says, would wander far, far away from where my actions, my heart and spirit have taken me, if it means being brought home renewed, cleansed and prepared for what lies ahead in my life, then it shall be worth whatever sacrifice God asks of me. Would you journey into the wilderness if God called you there for a while? We would be in good company as many have gone there before us. The Israelites wandered in the wilderness for forty years, Job spent time there as did John the Baptist, Paul and Jesus; all of who came out renewed, invigorated, and prepared for the fulfillment of the rest of their life's work.

Isaiah 41:18 "I will open rivers on the bare heights, and fountains in the midst of the valleys. I will make the wilderness a pool of water, and the dry land springs of water." I will claim this promise; God will fill my spiritually dry self with Jesus Christ the living water. He will turn the dryness that fills my mouth with dust into pools of words rushing out as rivers of revelation. I gladly rush into my wilderness knowing with all faith that the time is right, the Holy Spirit goes with me, and God's will for my life will be attained by the act.

# NINE

## Homesick

Remember that homesick feeling when you were a kid at summer camp; that sinking sensation in the pit of your stomach that you were all alone in a room of strange people? I still get that; call it an emotion, as I occasionally long for home. A desire not for my childhood house but just the recognized scenery, the faces of people I have known all my life, and for that rushing awareness of all things familiar. Moving away from Southampton County fourteen years ago I knew that I was choosing to let my past remain there and that my future would lie securely in my new home. It seems lately that this homesick feeling has been weighing upon my spirit more often than in a long time.

Let me be clear. I love it here in the New River Valley. The people are warm, friendly and I have made lots of friends, one who is of the very best caliber, with others closely following; I have a brother and his family two counties away which is a tremendous blessing. The scenery is breathtaking, the opportunities abound, yet it is still not really home, at least not in the same way as my childhood hometown and those encompassing memories are to me.

Homesick. I was just through my old hometown a couple of weeks ago where I visited the restaurant where I worked for almost twenty years, seeing several old friends and visiting family too. Maybe it is more of a nostalgic feeling that I am aware of now, bringing me to this homesick emotion since I so recently traveled back to where my childhood and adolescence was so very special and the raising of my own family seemed to be perfectly set in our hometown.

Whatever the cause for this emotional missive, I am missing the meandering back roads; the gallant spreads of farmland with row upon row of corn, peanuts and cotton, the rivers, the main street, country charm and the welcoming friends. I love driving through this small city's main thoroughfare, named Clay Street, where the houses are magnificent, the yards immaculate, and the memories of riding my bike up and down to the park and friends houses never fails to put a smile on my face.

Am I homesick for a feeling or longing desire? Maybe I am, or I may be feeling homesick for memories sake. Whichever the reason I will shake it off, look around at this new home I have made, count my blessings and know that as always I can say it is well with my soul.

# TEN

# Tracking

My sister gave me an odometer to wear so I might keep track of the steps in my day, and I can see how it would make one's performance improve as you want to outdo each day's numbers. It is similar to walking on my treadmill, I am always hoping for a few extra calories burned, another minute more and as many steps as possible added to the previous walk. So, what else do we track through our lives?

If you are in business you would track your financials, expenses, sales, clients, mileage on your vehicle and earnings. If you are a parent you might track your child's growth and teeth loss, when they took first steps and spoke their first words, you would also track their progress through school with report cards, pictures and scrapbooking. A student tracks their grades, their syllabus and sporting events. The average person tracks their savings, health, diet, and time. As a writer I track my characters, timelines, events and chapters. My husband and I track whose turn it is to drive when on trips as we change positions every hour and half or so.

Often we track without thought as it becomes ingrained into our minds as simply part of who we have become; we are trackers. Consider our ancestors for a moment. As we look back through time we find that yes, they tracked too. Without their own particular sort of tracking we would not have the Word in the form we have it today. From the Hebrews sharing story after story to their children thousands of years ago to the early Christians saving for holy prosperity the letters of the apostles, we recognize tracking at its core. Tracking history, tracking faith, tracking God's plans for His kingdom and His people.

Time marches on whether we are consciously tracking it or not. Most, if not all, of us do track time, based on the twenty four hour day, the week, and the year. We watch time tick away at work or anticipating an event, we mark time with anniversaries and holidays, and we track it all together calling it life. If I tracked the time I waste I suspect it would be more than I care to admit.

If I tracked my mistakes and sin I would be ashamed. If I tracked the number of times I have been forgiven the number would be infinite. Tracking God's mercy in my life is similar to the odometer my sister gave me to track my steps as I want to continually do better, make my spiritual life stronger and more influential than the day before. Now that is something worth tracking.

# ELEVEN

## "It's not whether you win or lose its how you play the game."

What game are you playing or do you think that you have your life all under control? Remember the kid's game, The Game of Life? The roll of the dice determined whether you had success or failure, a big family or none at all. In reality we really cannot afford to leave our future to chance, it is much too important not to have a game plan. In the end it will be a combination of how you played the game, who and what you believed in, and how you treated others. Sounds simple, but in actuality it is much more difficult to accomplish a complete round of this game called life.

How do you play your game of life? Do you follow a set of rules, carefully and purposely committing to a course of action for how you think and your expectations? Or do you throw caution to the wind, letting life happen in a "what will be, will be" fashion? This is the part where it really does matter how you play the game because this will determine whether you win or lose. Following the rules means submitting to a higher authority, God, and His rules found in His Word. This is how you win the game. The rules I am talking about, condensed they are the "Ten Commandments", are definitely the most important part of the play book. There are also those rules followed that we find all throughout the scriptures. I am referring to the conviction of God through the Holy Spirit, as He directs us according to His plan for how we are to live and treat one another directly from the apostles found in the New Testament.

What about the unexpected that often happens, how do we fit that into our game? You think everything is on track for what you have planned and boom, it falls in all around you; your well laid out plans for an orderly life are squashed by the surprise that can often come upon us suddenly and without warning. Have you ever experienced vertigo? It is an odd spinning sensation caused by crystals in your ear canal shifting. I hit my head a few days ago, and three days later I experienced vertigo for the first time. My heart was pounding, my world was spinning, and I could not regain control over it. The sensation had to run its course and there was little I could do but take Dramamine for the nausea. This is how it feels when disaster strikes and you feel like you have lost the ability to stay on the course of your life's game plan, everything is spinning out of control. Does this mean we should have a backup plan? Yes, a definite yes to always having a backup plan, but more than that, we need to have a God plan. He alone can prevent us from losing our game to the "vertigo" that might try to spin our world around.

The game of life is no board game, nor is it win, lose or draw. There is a way to secure a win by looking towards our Creator for His plans, playing the right way, making good informed choices, and following the rules that God has given to us in His Word. It truly matters how you play the game yet it also truly matters that you win. Take time to seek

His will for your life, have a backup plan in case of "vertigo", and by all means treat life like the serious thing it is, not a game, but reality.

# TWELVE

## Our Heart's Theme

Psalms 45:1 "My heart overflows with a pleasing theme; I address my verses to the king; my tongue is like the pen of a ready scribe."

What theme is flowing from your heart today? Is it one of grace and love or is it bitterness and envy? Is your "pleasing theme" one that reveals your thanksgiving for all that God has done for you or does it show an unrepentant spirit? Every new day gives us opportunity to change that theme, turning a life filled with darkness into one radiating light. I, more than some, may have the gift of pen to write my theme in honor of my King, but the pen is not the only way to express our hearts and souls. We honor our Lord by attitude, gratitude and service, allowing the love of God to be revealed through our willingness to be who God intended for us to be.

I am blessed to be able to share my heart and spirit in this way, with pen and paper; yet I understand that there is much more that I can do to express my love for my Savior. My life remains an open book, my actions, reactions and interactions reveal what I believe and how willing I am to let others see what I know to be the truth. Storms may rage through our lives at times, yet we can hold onto our "pleasing themes" as we trust in God who knows our hearts and minds, and brings us out of the darkness and into the light.

Lifting up our praise and worship through our lives expressing our "pleasing theme" due to the amazing love and mercy of our God, our Father, our King. Whether through pen and paper, song, teaching, leading or simply living, we show the world where our hearts truly lie; securely in the arms of God.

# THIRTEEN

## Choices

I have just returned from a work trip where I stayed with my sister and her husband. They graciously allow me to use their home as a base while I work, sleeping in their guest room. The first morning after I arrived my sister innocently asked me how I slept. I had to be honest and told her that I really had not slept good at all. She was surprised of course, because I usually sleep really well at her house. I had to tell her the reason why I had not this particular time saying, "there were no sheets on the bed." The look on her face was hilarious as comprehension on what had occurred took place. My brother-in-law had pulled the comforter up without sheets and then forgotten to go back and remake the bed. She asked why I had not gotten them out of bed to help, but I had not wanted to wake up the entire house and myself by turning on lights and foraging through closets and drawers for sheets.  I was able to find a pillow case in the dark and at least had a cool spot to lay my head.

We had a good laugh and that evening at her ladies ministry meeting we repeated the story so everyone could enjoy the chuckle. One of her friends shared her way of solving the sheet problem with her guest house. She leaves two choices out on the unmade bed, a cotton and a silk, for her company to make on their own. Brilliant! Give them a choice! Would you prefer the choice of putting on your own sheets or having someone choose them for you? Of course the choosing means you would make your own bed in this case.

This brings to mind the choices that we make and the wisdom of God for allowing us the freedom to do so. Would we rather not have to choose between right and wrong, or what decisions we make? It seems so much better to have the opportunity to make our independent choices, so even if we make a mistake we can learn and distinguish between what we did and what we should have done. Do we choose silk sheets or plain cotton and do we even know which we would rather have or does it depend on the situation? Which one makes us comfortable and which one can we live with while we experience the consequences of our decisions?

My sister's husband did not intentionally leave the sheets off the bed and yet by doing so it set off a chain reaction of decisions that had to be dealt with such as whether or not I slept with or without sheets for a night and whether or not I tell my sister or find my own sheets for the following nights. Things we do, whether on purpose or by accident, can cause an avalanche of reactions. I hope to always make wise decisions, making the best choices, praying over the hard ones and even the not so hard ones. I believe I would rather have two things to choose from, silk or cotton, than to have my choices made by someone else, or to not have any choices at all.

# FOURTEEN

## Making the Extraordinary

While packing for an upcoming trip I found myself gathering items almost randomly, as I chose what to put in my bags. I did not have to think too hard. I travel so often that it takes little to no effort to accomplish the preparation. I started thinking about all the things I do in this way, with very little attention, as it has become almost rote memorization. I am sure that I often miss out on many opportunities during the day as I mechanically rush through, focused not on my tasks at hand, but maybe (as a writer) daydreaming about the next chapter in my latest book or something as mundane as what I am cooking for dinner. Considering now all the daily routines that become thoughtless actions, such as packing for a trip, I have discovered, hopefully not too late, that much of my life has been spent in the ordinary instead of the extraordinary.

What exactly do I need to do to ensure the extraordinary happens as often as the ordinary? It will be different every day, circumstances change, opportunities arise, people come and go; my eyes will need to be open and prepared for these things that go beyond the average routine of my day. I believe that there is a purpose for each new day to become a point in time that will make my ordinary become extraordinary. One thing we all eventually learn is that the older we get the faster time goes and it can fly past. We wake up one morning and realize not only how much of our life is behind us, but for some of us, we understand that very little time is left to accomplish all that we had wanted. I ask myself now, is what I have been, what I have done and what I have planned, enough? Is my life like the suitcase I blindly pack without giving any real thought as to what I am putting into it? Has it become so routine that I barely give a thought to what I am doing, what I throw together to make up a day?

I want to live an extraordinary life. I want to pay close attention to what goes into every moment and what I can take away from each one. I know that there are many lost days which I will never get back but with every new dawn there is an amazing opportunity for the ordinary to become extraordinary. When I pack for my next trip I may still do so with little thought, randomly tossing in one item of clothing after another, this is probably true. That is not so important as making the journey I am preparing for become memorable. In the same way I can continue my daily routine without too much change of what I am doing but definitely thinking about changing how I do it to make the ordinary become extraordinary.

# FIFTEEN

## My Rock

Psalms 18:2 "The LORD is my rock and my fortress and my deliverer, my God, my rock, in whom I take refuge, my shield, and the horn of my salvation, my stronghold."

Facing the dawn of another day, my spirit is lifted up to receive peace and hope, with a steadfast belief that God has already prepared a way for me before my eyes have even opened. No matter the substance of what this day holds, I firmly and faithfully place my hope in the God of my life. He is my Rock, the foundation that my entire being, from soul to heart and from mind to spirit, is dependent upon and there is no fear in me. My existence longs for one thing; to bring glory to my Lord and Savior. Everything that I am and do centers around this. Knowing what He has done and will do for me, how could I do anything else?

Today, just as every day, I believe that my refuge, my salvation, my stronghold, lies securely in the hands of God. The storms may come, surely they will come, but this I know, the protection of my great God will never end and He will see me through them all. Today is a day of peace and hope, the storms may linger on the horizon, but I have no fear for I stand on the promise of the cross. There was I time when I depended on myself to get through each day. The power and beauty of salvation, the peace and joy of love and the strength and wisdom of the Holy Spirit has given me everything I need to count on God.

My prayer is that through my story, my witness, someone who needs the Rock of salvation, the Stronghold and Shield, will come across this message and turn to God to see them through all the days of their lives, the mornings filled with peace and the storms on their horizons as well. Seek peace not war, love not hate, hope instead of frustration, and choose life and not death. God will then be all you need, and more.

# SIXTEEN

## Honest Testimony

We all carry burdens around, life can be hard. Sometimes difficulties arise because of our own sins and because of our unwillingness as believers to share with those who need to hear. To keep hidden away, often locked deeply inside of ourselves, those things we have struggled with, can be as detrimental to our own lives as it is to those who desperately need to hear what we have been through, but due to our silence will never know. We must remove our masks of "holier than thou" and replace them with "been there, done that."

The testimony of Paul from Acts chapter twenty-two: "And I said, 'Lord, they themselves know that in one synagogue after another I imprisoned and beat those who believed in you. And when the blood of Stephen your witness was being shed, I myself was standing by and approving and watching over the garments of those who killed him.'" Paul's witness was his history of wrongdoing against those same people who he wanted to not only belong to, but to lead. Do you and I have the courage to stand among our peers and say, there but by the grace of God go I? Can we allow the Holy Spirit to lead us where we have always been afraid to go? Can we venture out into the darkness of the world to share with sinners our own unjustified sin, revealing that our hearts are pure only through the blood of Jesus Christ?

I have been where you are, I have hurt as you are hurting, I have sinned as you are sinning, and I know the burdens that you are struggling through. This is the message that is missing in a world where the lost are seeking a safe place to turn. It is the healing touch of, I understand you, I get you, both which are missing from the voice of those claiming victory in Christ and yes admittedly it is a message that I must believe has been missing from some of my own ministry. Declaring victory is one thing but standing to fight the good fight with the victory of Jesus Christ as our battle flag is completely different. Reaching the lost with compassion and understanding can be accomplished with truth, clarity and honest testimony.

We are remiss in our walk as Christians if we fail to relay the message of redemption through the forgiveness of our own sins. I have been disobedient in many ways throughout the years. I have lied, ignored the urging of the Holy Spirit, I have been unforgiving for too long in some relationships and have committed so many other sins that it would shock some who are closest to me. I refuse to air them all here today but when the Holy Spirit leads me to share with those I am witnessing too I would be sinning not to do so. Are you trying to deal alone with struggles, burdens, pain or conflict? If you are not sure of your relationship with Jesus, or if you are going through storms that happen to us all at some time or another, reach out to someone who cares and will pray with and for you. If you know someone struggling, then reach out to them with love, care and prayer.

# SEVENTEEN

## Follow Through

What happens after the sermon is over, the last hymn sung, the last prayer lifted? Do we, the lay people, the teachers, the choir members, and yes even the pastors, go about the rest of the week forgetting what we have experienced? I think it sometimes does go that way, but more often I believe that Christians are going out, refueled, sharing what they have heard, what they have been fed. Here may be where we fall short though, we do not "follow through."

What happens after I write a devotion, post it and move on? I have come to recognize that my writing ministry does not end with the push of the enter key on my computer. It does not stop when I have added it to my book of devotions in its file folder, nor does it end with those who like my posts and comment on them; it is through these moments that my writing ministry begins. I always hope to have planted seeds with my words, my vision. God has shown me that I must indeed go a huge step further and "follow through" with those I have touched, watering and weeding the seeds until they become fruit.

What would have happened if Peter, John and the other disciples had not carried on with the gospel of Jesus Christ, not "followed through?" Are you with me on this point? Without their courage and inspiration to spread the Word, Jesus Christ, the good news of salvation would have died on the cross, been resurrected and ascended into Heaven with our Lord. If we have no "follow through" on the seeds we have planted, at least to go back occasionally and check to see that they are watered and are taking root, our ministries, or the seeds we plant, will die. The Kingdom cannot grow without the "follow through."

Where does the power come from to continue to plant, water, and harvest? Our strength is found only in the Lord. No, we cannot simply walk away from the seeds and expect God to do the rest but we can turn to Him for strength to endure. 2 Corinthians 9:6 "The point is this: whoever sows sparingly will also reap sparingly, and whoever sows bountifully will also reap bountifully." Hard work and implementation, listening to where the Holy Spirit is leading us, these things will see us far when we are "following through" with our planting.

Planting the seeds is not enough. We must be willing to become the tools that God uses to continue the work until the harvest is ready for reaping keeping in mind that it is only through God that there is any growth. Looking deeper into scripture we find:

1 Corinthians 3:6 "I planted, Apollos watered, but God gave the growth."

2 Corinthians 9:10 "He who supplies seed to the sower and bread for food will supply and multiply your seed for sowing and increase the harvest of your righteousness."

1 Corinthians 3:7 "So neither he who plants nor he who waters is anything, but only God who gives the growth."

God has revealed through His Word that the importance of our ministries is the "follow through." That planting the seeds is only the first step in the process of growth and harvesting, keeping in mind that the growth comes from God's power and strength. We must be willing to go all the way, to "follow through" not only when the opportunity presents itself to us but in all circumstances.

## EIGHTEEN

## I'm not enough

I'm not good enough...I'm not liked enough...I'm not smart enough or pretty enough...I'm not spiritual enough, I'm not enough...

What "I'm not enough" are you battling with in private? Do not let it keep you imprisoned, afraid to be who you are meant to be, doing what you are meant to do. Satan would have you believe that your talents and abilities, your gifts, will never be enough. He would have you think that you do not measure up against the world around you and unfortunately it is way too easy to fall into his trap. It is all a lie. Let me tell you what I know to be true.

God knows you from inside out, top to bottom and head to toe; He created each of us and is intimately familiar with who we are and what we will become. "For you formed my inward parts; you knitted me together in my mother's womb. I praise you, for I am fearfully and wonderfully made. Wonderful are your works; my soul knows it very well." Psalms 139:13-14

The "I'm not enough" cry reaches far into Heaven and to the ears of our God. He searches our innermost hearts, in places where no one else can see. Our great God not only knows us but He is completely aware of our every thought, desire and movement or lack thereof. "I'm not enough" will never be acceptable to Him because He created you for something greater than being compared to anyone else in the world. Psalms 139:1-2 "O LORD, you have searched me and known me! You know when I sit down and when I rise up; you discern my thoughts from afar."

"I'm not enough" are words that you beloved should never utter as a believer in Jesus Christ as you are so much more than enough. You are a new creation. You are enough for Him, empowered by Him, enlightened and made boldly and greatly in the image of God. 2 Corinthians 5:17 "Therefore, if anyone is in Christ, he is a new creation. The old has passed away; behold, the new has come."

"I'm enough" should become your battle cry, your decree, your mantra. As you grow in the Spirit, walking in the light of Jesus, you will know without a doubt that you are enough. You are called to a higher purpose bought with the blood of Christ, who says to you dear brother, dear sister, that you are indeed enough.
Romans 8:28 "And we know that for those who love God all things work together for good, for those who are called according to his purpose."

"I'm not enough" is never going to be true for you as a child of the King. "I'm not enough" is a lie in a world that knows only darkness. For the world there is never enough. For God you are always enough, as He has bid you come, just as you are. Matthew 11:28-30 "Come to me, all who labor and are heavy laden, and I will give you rest. Take my yoke upon you, and learn from me, for I am gentle and lowly in heart, and you will find rest for your souls. For my yoke is easy, and my burden is light."

# NINETEEN

## The Eternal Caregiver

I sat watching a mother bird feed her three babies that had fallen from their nest underneath the eaves of our garage. They have been in our yard and our lives for about four days now. My husband has felt like a worried father; he checked on them hourly from the moment we discovered them first out of the safety of their nest. They have responded to him to the point of following him, almost as a mother duck has her babies waddling after her. He has continually checked on them, often going outside with the pretense of one thing or another, but in actuality going to see his birds. It is so beautiful to watch the care in his heart for these three babies as his concerns for their safety and growth has manifested itself in his obvious attention to them.

The mother bird has worked at the feeding of her babies all day. Bringing and depositing into their open empty mouths a meal of worms or bugs, then resolutely flying off to seek out more nourishment to sustain them. This mother bird was a dedicated parent, providing for and loving her children. This went on for two or three days and eventually the birds were able to maneuver themselves around and even separated in our yard. Never was the mother out of sight for any length of time nor did she lose her focus on them. As I sat silently watching, studying her actions, I saw that she went from one to another and back again until she had fed them all. This continuous care for her children was unceasing and it was a testament of her love and sense of responsibility. Today the birds are mature enough to open their wings and hop upon the patio furniture, revealing they will soon fly away. Mother has done her best. She has cared for her children.
Now it is time to let them go.

God cares for each of us, his children, much in the same way, when we accept Him as our Father. He would be our eternal Caregiver. He will feed us with His Word, bless us with His grace, and love us with an unending stream of hope and goodness.

"Consider the ravens: they neither sow nor reap, they have neither storehouse nor barn, and yet God feeds them. Of how much more value are you than the birds!" Luke 12:24

"The young lions suffer want and hunger; but those who seek the LORD lack no good thing." Psalms 34:10

"For the LORD God is a sun and shield; the LORD bestows favor and honor. No good thing does he withhold from those who walk uprightly." Psalms 84:11

These are just a few of the scriptures from God's Word revealing His care for each of us who claim Him as our Father. God created us for this. His love is abundant, His grace is sufficient, His mercy is everlasting. We will always need God's care that in itself is an never ceasing gift from our Father. As we grow in knowledge and grace, we, as the baby birds are doing, can spread our wings and soar. Walking upright and securely in His protection, we can become all that He has intended for us to be. Isaiah 40:31 "but they who wait for the LORD shall renew their strength; they shall mount up with wings like eagles; they shall run and not be weary; they shall walk and not faint." The difference between God's attention to His creation and this mother bird's to her babies is His caring never ceases, no matter how far away we might fly from Him.

# TWENTY

## Miscarriage

Miscarriage is often a silent and lonely grief, with most women not discussing it once they have recovered. I know several who have lost children this way, including myself and it is rare to bring up the experience. It hurts. I was just reminded how it felt while watching a television program where a young lady was struggling to have a child. The emotional impact was severe as the memories came flooding back. Why the silent struggle? For me it has always been based on one thing; unlike other losses there is no memory attached to a miscarried child. No fond glimpses into the past of a life of any kind, no life, no memories.

It was about a year ago that I came to terms with the death of my baby. It had occurred in 1977 and had taken me all this time to begin to deal with it. Guilt. Guilt for not grieving. Guilt for allowing even one day to go by without remembering. Guilt for allowing thirty seven years to come and go without dealing with it. The process was overwhelming yet so good for my heart and soul. God helped me see that grief has no timetable. My feelings were my own. In order to enable myself to understand the emotions associated with the loss I had needed the time, all the time that it took.

Looking back at my immaturity when I had my miscarriage I see how I can now more easily understand the magnitude of loss than I did as a young woman of nineteen. I was not prepared then to grasp the impact of the death. To accept that the baby, my child, would forever have a place in my heart, to realize that someday I would indeed know my child, and to constantly think about what he or she could have become in this life, was too much of a concept for me then. God had appointed a time for acceptance and it has been a beautiful experience.

I am led to write this today, Memorial Day, as I think that it has become, at least for me, a day to remember not just our patriots but also our loved ones who have passed. I never held my baby, never saw my child, but I know that infant was a part of me for four months before going on to be held in the arms of Jesus. It is hard to write. It still hurts. I am grieving. And now I am at last able to talk about the miscarriage, to share with those who have experienced this same kind of loss, and in this way I can begin my own healing.

Psalm 73:26 "My flesh and my heart may fail, but God is the strength of my heart and my portion forever."

# TWENTY-ONE

# Judgmental

I saw that a church in Florida had posted on their sign outside the following: "homosexuals repent or go to hell." I was hurt at the angry and judgmental words and cannot imagine what a Christian leader must be thinking to put those thoughts up on a board for everyone to see. Why not put: murderers repent, abortionist repent, liars, adulterers, unbelievers, repent or go to hell? If you believe that any sin needs to be repented of then you must believe that all sin must be repented. The only way to do that is through the acceptance of Jesus Christ and allow his blood to wash you clean. We live in a world where most people who do not follow the truth of Christ believe that sin is only sin when it involves hurting someone else, that your private life is just that, yours. I believe that our lives, both public and private belong to God the Father who gives breath to every living thing and it is to him we will answer for unrepentant sins not to one another. You may not believe the way I do but that is no reason for me to be rude, there is more reason for me to love you and show you why.

Titus 3:3-5 tells us exactly how we should act towards one another, especially when it comes to the matter of approaching unbelievers. "For we ourselves were once foolish, disobedient, led astray, slaves to various passions and pleasures, passing our days in malice and envy, hated by others and hating one another. But when the goodness and loving kindness of God our Savior appeared, he saved us, not because of works done by us in righteousness, but according to his own mercy, by the washing of regeneration and renewal of the Holy Spirit." If we who once were unloved to the point of being unlovable, who felt the judgmental finger of hate and blame, cannot understand how others feel and be gentle in our approach to them, who will?

It is the responsibility of every Christian to reveal to the world the face of God. God is not revealed through the pointed finger of judgment but with the open heart and arms of love found in Jesus Christ. Let the church proclaim repentive love, not pointed hate, showing the truth that before we first believed we all fell short of the glory of God. Romans 3:23-24 "For all have sinned and fall short of the glory of God, and are justified by his grace as a gift, through the redemption that is in Christ Jesus." Maybe that church in Florida (or any church) should put on their sign something like, "God loves us all, come in and find out how much and why."

# TWENTY-TWO

# Technology

A curse and a blessing are what I have come to understand about certain things in this age of "technology". Life has enough distractions on its own without me adding to them with something like, let's say, my cell phone. It is a blessing because I can sit comfortably on my couch writing this piece without having to hold a bulky laptop on my lap or go to the office and sit at my desk to write. It can be a curse due to the temptations it puts in front of me; to check Facebook, to read texts while driving (never answer them), playing games when I should be doing anything else (yes, words with friends), and to constantly be looking for email. There are some wonderful advantages to my phone too; a big one is having my bible at my fingertips and my Kindle for reading. A blessing and a curse, those are the facts behind the distractions of my cell phone.

There are other distractions in life too; those that keep me from being everything that I know God expects me to be and doing all that he has planned for my life. One big one is the television that seems to be on twenty-four seven, (by my husband's choice), and though I have learned to tune it out, at times I am drawn to what is on the screen, the news especially. When I could be into the Word, writing or meditating, I often find myself being pulled away by the things around me, the television by far not the only thing. The list of distractions will grow longer as I add to it: the housework, the magazine beckoning to be thumbed through, the constant ringing of the phone, yet these are everyday distractions that we all face. What about the distractions of the spiritual sort?

Satan has distractions just waiting to be put in the way of our spiritual lives, anything that will take us away from our ministries, take away our joy, and move us away from our fellowship with God. He uses other people, he uses our jobs, our families and even ourselves to lead us from fruitful days, pull us away from our ministries and most importantly our focus on God. When we are least aware of the distractions of the world, we are more likely to succumb to them. One moment we are busily going about our life's work and without warning, something, a mishap, mistake, accident, or something of the world, jumps out at us. We get knocked off course by these distractions and the only way to keep this from having a lasting impact on our lives is too shake them off, moving boldly forward with the assurance that God is with us. His voice in our hearts is never a distraction, it is our mainstay, and it is the force that drives us.

Whether they be curse or blessing, the distractions of this world must be overcome by the power within us that is the Holy Spirit, Jesus Christ, who we emulate. 1 Corinthians 7:35 "I say this for your own benefit, not to lay any restraint upon you, but to promote good order and to secure your undivided devotion to the Lord." Order is exactly what is missing at times when we find ourselves too easily distracted. I try to plan my days in advance, work, church, social, and family, all checked marked on a list in my mind's eye. I keep a calendar on my phone and on my desk too, to ensure that nothing distracts from my remembering and performing well. Order, where is God in the order of my day, my life? I pray to never again, yes it has happened many times, allow the temptations of this world to distract and take me away from my journey through this life in God's will, and with His plans.

# TWENTY-THREE

## Getting Life Done

I was watching some construction going on across the street from my home when I noticed this one man walking to and fro around the property. It intrigued me enough so that I continued to watch him for a few minutes and he really never did anything, that I could see, was not overseeing the job by the looks of it and never spoke to anyone else. Now, before you judge me for being a nosy neighbor, I want to justify my gaping at the view from my window because I was taking a break from work and actually sitting on my sofa, so this scene unfolded practically in front of my very eyes. Anyway the idea of the running around, back and forth with getting nothing done brought to mind how often this seems to happen in my spiritual life.

I have a routine that I try to stick with every day, even when traveling; it consists of bible reading, a few minutes of study, praying, meditating, and writing and then on to whatever my schedule has on it for the day. During the course of this scheduled time I rush back and forth to check email, voicemail, writing in between chores, back to working on business with a pause for lunch and maybe a little more writing. Sounds crazy but I am struck by the idea of trying to decipher how much and what I am actually accomplishing during this to and fro, back and forth lifestyle I have found myself in. I know that we need routine to keep our lives in check, but honestly, I have to wonder if I am somewhat like the man across the street, really getting little if anything done.

I do not want to interject a list of my deeds, good or bad or even both here, so let it be sufficient to say that the company I represent seems satisfied, my family is happy with the results of my contributions and I believe I am working very hard with the ministries I have chosen to lead. So why then would I feel as if something is missing or being left undone, what is this hollow part of me that feels like for all the scurrying around I am not getting anywhere? So maybe the time has come to look a little closer at where my heart and spirit are and not merely look for a series of what things I have done or will eventually get finished.

Things of the spirit are going in the complete opposite direction of the things of the world and what my heart is saying to me now is to not make what I am accomplishing in my "daily" life a competition with my spiritual life and what that might mean to the culmination of who and what I am. My innermost thoughts and feelings are unreadable to anyone but myself and God, as are everyone's. This feeling of rushing to and fro without seeing any results (for my spiritual life) is a product of my own expectations based on what I see other people doing and God says to me, run your own race girl! 1 Corinthians 9:24 "Do you not know that in a race all the runners run, but only one receives the prize? So run that you may obtain it."

So the gentleman who I was watching across the street is now gone on to other things I assume since he is no longer pacing around the neighbor's yard. He will never know that even if he did not accomplish a single thing during his day (and maybe he did), he was an inspiration for me. He inspired me to write this piece and he inspired me to take a look at what the routine of rushing to and fro, back and forth, around in circles, eventually comes to yield in my life, my heart and my spirit. My spiritual growth is a mystery unknown to any accept me and God yet the fruits of my life may be made known to a few or many, this I leave in the hands of God.

# TWENTY-FOUR

# Spring Cleaning

Spring cleaning; some people face this challenge around this time of year and to each and every one of us it means something different yet it is the same. I clean out my closets, maybe for you it's dresser drawers, my husband does exterior I do interior, yet we all are accomplishing the exact same goal, cleaning up, or tossing out the old and freshening the leftover. The time is definitely right for some clearing away of the cobwebs in the attic and in the garage as well. There is so much we can do to spruce up our property inside and out, preparing it for use in the warmer weather months and to relax with open windows and screen doors to enjoy the springtime weather. Our hearts, minds, and spirits can use a little spring cleaning too, and so I chose some scripture that will assist us in doing just that.

1 John 1:9 "If we confess our sins, he is faithful and just to forgive us our sins and to cleanse us from all unrighteousness." This is the perfect prescription for how to begin spring cleaning ourselves; the cleansing away of our sins. Let us be real right now, as we all have something to confess, get off our chest so to speak; clean yourself of this dark stain on your spirit by laying it down at the altar asking forgiveness and mercy and getting rid of any unrighteousness once and for all.

2 Corinthians 5:17 "Therefore, if anyone is in Christ, he is a new creation. The old has passed away; behold, the new has come." If we believe in Jesus as Lord and Savior we are new. Being made completely new is as clean as one can get, and I praise God as he has given us a way to never need spring cleaning again in this particular form. Believe on Jesus, be made into a new creation, let the old pass away, and the saving grace of God will wash away your sins forever. When you toss out the old things from your attic or garage you do not go chasing down the trash truck to get them back, so neither will you desire the old life once you have been made new in Christ.

Philippians 4:8 "Finally, brothers, whatever is true, whatever is honorable, whatever is just, whatever is pure, whatever is lovely, whatever is commendable, if there is any excellence, if there is anything worthy of praise, think about these things." There is the perfect way to spring clean your spirit; think only these praise worthy thoughts and not only your mind but your heart and spirit will overcome any negativity, fear, or discouragement. Open up those windows, let the fresh air and sunshine come rushing in, feels wonderful, does it not?

Ephesians 4:22-23 "To put off your old self, which belongs to your former manner of life and is corrupt through deceitful desires, and to be renewed in the spirit of your minds." The putting away of your old self is like taking a bag of old clothes to Goodwill knowing that you will never see them again or have need of them; now the old self is gone and you are transformed from a sinful nature to one of righteousness. Once again we find that what is old and used up is replaced with something beautiful and everlasting, you need not be ashamed, you have been completely washed clean.

Are you feeling the need to do some personal spring cleaning? When you wipe away the dirt that has been building up and smearing your windows and your view, you can see much clearer what you have been missing. The same happens when you are washed clean by the blood of Jesus Christ, you can now see clearly what your life has been missing. Take some time from doing your spring cleaning to wipe away the cobwebs of your mind, lift your spirits and know that the burdens of your heart can be rolled away for good.

# TWENTY-FIVE

## Let Me Be A Witness

I am a witness to Jesus Christ; no I have never laid eyes upon his body but I have seen him through the miracles that are everywhere I look, and in the lives of countless other believers who have shared their testimony, their experiences, and their witness. What exactly is a witness? The definition of witness is to give or serve as evidence of, testify to; this is its meaning as a verb. To use as a noun, to be a witness, simply add "the one who" to the words and you have in its totality, a witness, the one who gives evidence to. Therefore I conclude that I am a witness as I testify to the truth of Jesus in my life, my heart, soul, and spirit.

Psalm 40:3 "He put a new song in my mouth, a song of praise to our God. Many will see and fear, and put their trust in the LORD." How will many see, many fear, without our witness? When we eagerly share all the marvelous things that God has done for us, singing his praises, our witness becomes what brings others to believe. A new song, one that sweetly proclaims that God is sovereign over my life and by his grace and mercy I am thriving in my ministry, in my witness.

Psalm 107:3-4 "Let the redeemed of the LORD say so, whom he has redeemed from trouble and gathered in from the lands, from the east and from the west, from the north and from the south." I am a witness; redeemed by the blood of Jesus Christ and must be willing to share his powerful work in my life in order to claim this title. Redeemed, disciple, believer, follower, witness; the words are different but each bears the same conviction that we will share the gospel in and throughout a dark, and growing darker world.

Isaiah 6:8 "And I heard the voice of the Lord saying, "Whom shall I send, and who will go for us?" Then I said, "Here am I! Send me." Yes! This should be my theme, here I am, send me! Yes! I will be a witness! I will give testimony to all the great things that God has done for me, how he saved me, redeemed me, loves me, blesses me, and yes, God will do the same for any who call on his name. Yes! I will be a witness to the glory of Christ who is living in me, who has transformed my life, fuels my ministry, and has taught me the most powerful and empowering lesson of all, love. This then, love, is my witness...

## TWENTY-SIX

## Spiritual Blues

I have been sick, really sick on the couch feeling bad; good news, I am better, not completely well but oh so much better. So much so that I kept my hair appointment today that I had postponed from over a week ago, cut and color. Since I wear my hair short I find it difficult to go more than four weeks without a cut so you can imagine how bad I looked, adding to that I have had this virus, so I no doubt doubled how awful I appeared. My stylist worked her magic as always and voila, I am looking more like my old cheerful self this evening. Of course, as many of life's moments do, this brought to mind a lesson of how our spirits may get rundown, needing some tender, loving, care just as our bodies, and yes, hair, need.

Have you ever felt like your spirit is down in the dumps, lackadaisical, even to the point of being unable to perform the task of everyday life? I am not talking depression, just the old fashioned, I can't help its; we all suffer from these times of needing a pick me up, spiritually and down deep within our souls. There is relief for our downtrodden spirits and it is found through our trust and faith in the Lord.  Isaiah 58:11
"And the Lord will guide you continually and satisfy your desire in scorched places and make your bones strong; and you shall be like a watered garden, like a spring of water, whose waters do not fail."

Similarly to how our physical appearance supports our emotional being, our spiritual health is assured by the healing hands of God.  In order for our life's ministries to grow and flourish we must have firm foundations; founded in the Word with faith, founded in prayer with meditation and communication with God and founded by a firm and solid relationship with Jesus Christ. To ensure our spiritual foundation is strong and secure we trust in the Lord for his healing mercy. His grace extends to our spirits as well as our bodies. Jeremiah 3:6 " Behold, I will bring to it health and healing, and I will heal them and reveal to them abundance of prosperity and security."

Just as my hair stylist saved the day for my physical appearance, the Lord is prepared to spiritually heal all his children. Psalm 34:18 "The Lord is near to the brokenhearted and saves the crushed in spirit." Those days of feeling spiritually down come to us all at some time or another, but the good news is that God has already prepared a way to lift our spirits, healing the hurt and struggling that we may be facing. There is a wonderful feeling that intensifies with an uplifted spirit, much like the happiness we discover after being sick for a long while. Giving all the glory for our healing spirit and the strengthening of our ministries to God, we may always be assured that by his loving grace we will continue on through the ups and downs of our lives.  2 Corinthians 12:9 "But he said to me, "My grace is sufficient for you, for my power is made perfect in weakness." Therefore I will boast all the more gladly of my weaknesses, so that the power of Christ may rest upon me."

## TWENTY-SEVEN

## Wearing Our Faith

Does our faith reflect who we really are to others? Our faith is revealed through our willingness to express our beliefs to others, through our actions and behavior in the world. I wear makeup to hopefully improve my looks, enhancing my face favorably so others will see the best of me. Am I wearing my faith in a similar way, to create an illusion of what I want others to see of me or am I truly using my faith to inspire those who I meet to see, not myself, but Jesus in me. Ephesians 3:16-17 "That according to the riches of his glory he may grant you to be strengthened with power through his Spirit in your inner being, so that Christ may dwell in your hearts through faith."

It is hard, this wearing of our faith, for it is tested every day as we face challenge after challenge, trials, temptations and not least of all, our own unwillingness to allow the world the opportunity to mock and smear our beliefs and our ministries.  As our very hearts and souls are left open for others to either accept, love, and most importantly come to see Jesus in us, we also leave ourselves open for the fulfillment of the Word. Isaiah 55:11 "So shall my word be that goes out from my mouth; it shall not return to me empty, but it shall accomplish that which I purpose, and shall succeed in the thing for which I sent it." We will face times of being lifted up and many more of being trod upon. But God has given us the same knowledge as the first believers had through his voice in the Word and here is where we allow our faith to grow and develop. James 1:3-4 " Count it all joy, my brothers, when you meet trials of various kinds, for you know that the testing of your faith produces steadfastness."

There is hope for those who believe and take their personal walk and ministry seriously; faith begins as a seed within that grows along with our spirit and love as we grow in knowledge and wisdom. As it grows we need never be concerned with the putting on of our faith as a woman puts on her makeup, because we will be wearing it as our anthem, with pride, conviction, and most of all courage. We are victorious because we have the faith to be victorious. 1John 5:4"For everyone who has been born of God overcomes the world. And this is the victory that has overcome the world-our faith."

# TWENTY-EIGHT

## Measuring Up

How do you measure your worth in God's kingdom as your personal convictions and conscious dictates? A good question to ask yourself is, "Does my life and ministry truly reflect Christ living in me?" I may ask, "Are my words merely the rambling of an overactive imagination or are they inspired by the Holy Spirit?" The answer may be found only when we seek God's will in our lives through prayer and meditation allowing God's Spirit to move in us and through His moving reveal exactly what we should be focused on. Ephesians 4:29 " Let no corrupting talk come out of your mouths, but only such as is good for building up, as fits the occasion, that it may give grace to those who hear."

We should constantly seek to remain focused on Jesus and the grace of God, the same grace that covered the first disciples, will cover our lives in such a way as to strengthen everything we are and do. This alone should encourage our hearts to fully accept the will of God and give us the boldness to realize that there is nothing keeping us from our personal ministry except our own unwillingness. The Holy Spirit is providing you and I with encouragement in a continuous flow of love and peace as we pray for discernment and clarity as to God's plans and our place within them. Romans 15:13 "May the God of hope fill you with all joy and peace in believing, so that by the power of the Holy Spirit you may abound in hope."

What does encouragement mean to your ministry or your spiritual life? Kind words of support will often reveal the reflection of the love of God back onto your life from those whom you seek to bless by your actions. Can you imagine being a preacher whose congregation never says "Great sermon!" Or a choir director who never feels appreciated by the choir or the audience? Who will lift us up with encouragement and support if we do not do so for one another? As believers we absolutely must be able to work courageously and stand firm in our faith in the righteous deeds we endeavor to do for God, yet I know that without encouragement we will be hard pressed to stay the course. Hebrews 10:25 " Not neglecting to meet together, as is the habit of some, but encouraging one another, and all the more as you see the Day drawing near."

Today I challenge myself, and you as well, to encourage at least one other person; someone who may be struggling in their spirit or in their ministry, to remind them to recognize and know the power of God upon their lives. Take some time also to look at where you measure up to the challenges that God has set before you to and open your heart to the conviction of God through the Holy Spirit.

# TWENTY-NINE

## The Gardens of Life

"The kiss of the sun for pardon, the song of the bird for mirth, one is nearer God's heart in a garden, than anywhere else on earth." Dorothy Francis Gurney

This poem is one I cross stitched and framed a long time ago while awaiting the birth of my second child. It's beauty and meaning has always been poignant to me most especially in the promise of spring. I have been blessed many times over with the opportunity to plant, tend, and harvest gardens, vegetable and flower alike. No other time is more important to the growth and harvest of a garden then springtime. To truly fulfill the promise of spring in all its glory we must be willing to put our hands into the rich dark soil, work it until it is weedless and free of rocks and thorns. Once we have the ground prepared we can then plant the seeds that will offer up their glorious blooms with the spring rains and warm sun needed to nurture and help them grow.

And now that we have planted our garden do we merely watch and wait to see the fruit of our work? No, we must be hardworking, good gardeners as we weed, fertilize and constantly tend our seeds until they sprout up from under the soil, little green stems reaching towards heaven, searching for the sun. Then with consistent and gentle care we tenderly assist with the growth of the plants until the promised blossoms are born.

Oh the kiss of the sun for pardon, the warmth of it on one's shoulder as you kneel on bended knees reveling in the touch of the good earth in your hands. Just as the plants need the sunlight for healthy production we too are in need, of the Son's light in order to lead productive lives as disciples. We are commissioned to plant the seeds of righteousness, hope, grace, mercy and love that will lead those who have yet to believe to not only do so but to become planters along with us. They too shall feel the kiss of the Son for pardon....

The song of the bird for mirth, where can you hear a lovelier sound than from the songbird in your garden? There is a sweetness like no other coming from the sounds of the song bird in spring. Song of Solomon 2:12 "The flowers appear on the earth, the time of singing has come, and the voice of the turtledove is heard in our land." When I am happy I sing; I sing songs of praise to God, happy little humming along songs of faith and joy. To hear the sound of birds in the spring is to bring awareness to our hearts that although we are not promised happiness every day, we can seek to at the least be inspired to some form of joy in life, particularly when we are enjoying the perimeter of our garden. As we work to create what one day will be an abundant harvest, we can find sweet momentum in the music from the songbird.

One is nearer God's heart in a garden rings truth to our awakening spirits as we see the evidence of our lives being fruitful as we harvest the souls from where we have planted our seeds of righteousness. As God walked through the Garden of Eden at the time of creation, I believe we can feel nearer to him as we work the ground, tend the seeds and eventually harvest our vegetables or flowers, and as we rejoice in the righteous harvest that is God's expectation of each of us, his chosen people, his Springtime planters, the song of his heart.

I observed some freshly plowed fields just the other day and it was decidedly one of the most vivid expressions of spring that I can remember seeing. I was aware of God's purpose for his creation, for me and for you, more acutely so than I ever have. We are commissioned by our great God to sow seeds of righteousness and to seek his grace and mercy so that he may in turn rain down upon our lives as never before. Just as the plowed fields beg for seed and nurturing to ensure growth our hearts can be the garden where God will plant his seeds of righteousness in each one of us.

Hosea 10:12 " Sow for yourselves righteousness; reap steadfast love; break up your fallow ground, for it is the time to seek the LORD, that he may come and rain righteousness upon you."

# THIRTY

## Umpa Love

I was having a conversation with my daughter the other day and was sharing that I was not feeling well, probably coming down with a bug; I was, am, sick with a nasty virus and chest cold. My nine year old grandson, Zachary, overheard the discussion and had the following good advice for his Nana; drink hot tea, eat some hot chicken soup, take a hot bath, and get some Umpa (his name for my husband) love. Out of the mouths of babes as they say; his implication of all things "hot" to assist me in getting back into good health did not go unnoticed even though he did not mean to lump his Umpa together in the category of "hot" but soothing, comforting. That then is the lesson of this story, what, where, and who do we turn to when we are sick, physically or spirituality? And an even deeper question, how sincerely do we offer these things?

Zachary's advice for me was for both my physical and emotional needs. He was thinking of all the things he knew would make me at least feel better if not cure me. The hot tea to soothe a sore throat, the hot chicken soup for my tummy, the hot bath for my aching body and the Umpa love for emotional support and comfort. His words of love have really done so much more than just make me smile; they have served to remind me of what loving one another as God loves us means. Reaching out to the sick, with a bowl of chicken soup and kind words, to the lonely with a visit and a cup of hot tea, and reaching out to comfort each other with open arms, Umpa love, these are how we meet the needs of the physically sick and emotionally downtrodden. But what about reaching out to the spirituality hurting, their needs are as real and cause as much pain and discomfort as any virus, chest cold, or combination thereof.

I am touched by my nine year old grandson's innocent yet mature insight to the needs of his grandmother who he loves very much. As we seek avenues to reach the world with the good news of the gospel, we can learn from this, as we know and obey God's greatest commandment, loving our neighbors as ourselves. I have, in my short writing ministry, written about this very thing often, loving ones neighbors. What I have taken away from my grandson's words is that when we say we love, we must mean we love, when we offer our gifts, we must be sincere, and when we share the gospel we must do so boldly and with kindness for those we hope to reach.

So, whether you see someone in need of a cup of tea to soothe their sore throat, in need of a bit of a bear hug to give them an emotional uplift, or if you know that someone who needs to hear the gospel, take time to show them you really do care enough to share what you can. In this ever darkening world we live in there is an awful lot of need to have revealed to it the real true love of Jesus Christ.

# THIRTY-ONE

## Winter is but a Memory

Winter is but a memory...Song of Solomon 2:11 "for behold, the winter is past; the rain is over and gone. The flowers appear on the earth, the time of singing has come, and the voice of the turtledove is heard in our land."

As we were driving across the New River Valley today on our way to church I made an innocent comment to my husband saying, "Winter is but a memory." The statement touched me deeply and felt very profound, so much it has impacted my entire day. I shared with several people today what springtime this year, more than other, is coming to mean to me. It is more than the new growth, though that is amazing to watch unfold as leaves bud out, it is more than the color, the smell or the warmth, it is the promise it brings to my heart, soul and spirit.

The seasons each hold blessings of individual proportion, blessings that are as unique to each of us as we are from different from one another. Winter's end brings with it a conclusion of darkness and cold, bitter winds and bare earth, holding the promise of all things warm, green and lush, a growing season for all things from flowers to grass and birth, as we see new life appearing all around. As the temperature outside soars, our hearts too rise with joy and excitement that Winter is but a memory.

This promise holds as well one that is the renewing of my soul with the truth of the peace of the gospel of Jesus Christ. I see where my discipleship through and for Him is going as I have placed all my hopes and expectations in the Lord, just as one hopes and expects in the spring's renewing of itself. My strength comes from knowledge which is the renewing of my mind in God's Word. A season of growth that continues on forever but is sparked into flames by spring's promise of the cold days passing into yesterday, Winter is but a memory.

Joel 2:23 "Be glad, O children of Zion, and rejoice in the LORD your God, for he has given the early rain for your vindication; he has poured down for you abundant rain, the early and the latter rain, as before."

Here then is another amazing promise of Spring, rain. Rain to promote growth in fresh turned fields, and rain that is needed to wash us clean and create in us a renewed covenant with God, all coming at a time when most needed. My spirit is lifted, my soul renewed with the promise of all that Spring has to offer, to my life, to the earth I love, and to the cleansing of my heart as it accepts the rain poured out from heaven.

Winter is but a memory...

# THIRTY-TWO

## Changing

I change my profile picture on Facebook like some people change their minds. We change bed sheets, baby's diapers, clothes, and countless other things almost every day. One thing that never changes, staying always constant, is God and his abundant love for us. He created us to be as changeable as he is unchanging. It is a wonderful thing to know that we can wake up to the unfailing awareness of our Father in Heaven who is never going to change. Malachi 3:6 "For I the LORD do not change; therefore you, O children of Jacob, are not consumed."

We continue on a path of change every day, making decisions that can be changed, aware of our feelings that are changing with every moment, and we can change our attitudes towards one another and towards God. All these things can be positive and hopefully fruitful, but we must be aware that they may be negative as well. Moving away from God and his plans for us, is the most negative change we could ever make. Change that brings about forgiveness instead of being unforgiving, change that makes our hearts long for more time with God and in his Word, not less, and making prayerful choices when it comes to decisions, these are the positives we can accentuate. Romans 12:2 " Do not be conformed to this world, but be transformed by the renewal of your mind, that by testing you may discern what is the will of God, what is good and acceptable and perfect."

My profile picture may change often but my ideals and beliefs will never change. I am committed to growing ever closer to my God, stronger in my spirit, and am hopeful for longevity in my writing ministry. The desire for change comes only when I realize that with growth and expansion of knowledge and experience I am choosing to better my life and to become more loving and understanding of those that I have contact with. That is good and acceptable change. What change has made a difference in your life lately? Has it been negative, and your heart desires to be renewed? Or, have you seen a positive change, maybe in attitude or understanding?  Ephesians 4:23-24 "and to be renewed in the spirit of your minds, and to put on the new self, created after the likeness of God in true righteousness and holiness."

# THIRTY-THREE

## Oasis

An oasis by definition is a pleasant or peaceful area in the midst of a hectic place or difficult situation. Once several years ago when driving through South Dakota I came across a beautiful oasis in the middle of what was miles and miles of prairie and desert. It was actually, oddly enough, named Al's Oasis; my husband's name is Al. Anyway, it was amazing coming up over a hill and suddenly there was a lake and lovely grassy area that literally took one's breath away so unexpectedly did you come upon it. While driving today I had a similar experience, as I took a highway that was unfamiliar to me, I suddenly came to a lake and surrounding it was a million (I exaggerate) Redbud trees in full bloom. I immediately recognized it for the oasis that it could have been if I had been in need of one.

Life sometimes gets dry, tasteless, tiresome, even boring, and these times can become difficult to deal with and get through, but thankfully God has set up oasis's for us along the way for us to stop, take refreshment, take a break, or simply take in the beauty of what he is doing for us. We find our places of peace in the essence of the earth, music, scripture, prayer, and at the altar. God will fill us with all we need to get through the dry days, just life your arms towards heaven and allow him to rain down his cleansing and healing water, your oasis.

Finding peace amidst a storm is welcome any day, but when the storm has completely blown us off course, even to the point of being lost in the pounding waves, it is significantly easier to battle through when offered an oasis from the trials. A place of peace or pleasant surroundings can be different for each of us, but as a man dying of thirst needs water from the desert oasis, we too need a place of quenching, refreshing water for our souls. Finding solace and comfort in a tempestuous situation can be compared to surviving a shipwreck, with the beach being your oasis.

Our Father has provided us with everything we could possibly need to calm the storms of life beginning and ending with prayer. Praying and being in fellowship with God can be the oasis welling up from within our own spirit as water springing up and into a river, becoming our saving grace when we are in need of it most. When we most need it he will provide us with the calm and peace that is balm for our weary spirits, a place of beauty, filled with grace and mercy. Not unlike the ones I have experienced unexpectedly while traveling, God knows what we need and provides us with our oasis when we may least expect them too.

Jeremiah 31:24 "For I will satisfy the weary soul, and every languishing soul I will replenish."

Mourning and lamenting denotes a closeness that comes from working together, living closely connected, and loving with an abiding feeling of oneness. This description of the women who had followed Jesus is telling of relationships that went so much further than mere listeners of Jesus, they loved him, they knew him personally and served him. And if they loved him, how much more deeply did Jesus love them, using them to minister to his needs, the disciples, and I am sure the many others who traveled with them all.

# FORTY-TWO

## Forgiveness

When asked by his brothers to forgive them for selling him into slavery Joseph's response was not exactly what mine would have been. His response? Genesis 50:19-20 "But Joseph said to them, "Don't be afraid. Am I in the place of God? You intended to harm me, but God intended it for good to accomplish what is now being done, the saving of many lives." So, let us take into consideration what the brothers had actually done to begin with: sold Joseph into slavery, lied to their father causing him to believe Joseph to be dead, caused a chain reaction of events that led Joseph to end in prison. But, the story did not end there. God had bigger plans and as Joseph himself said, it was to in the end save many lives.

Joseph recognized what we often forget or cannot see God's hands in everything. Our Father knows, He moves us, and uses us to bring to fruition all that He deems necessary for our own good and the good of the world. And yes, that includes those times we are hurt beyond our understanding by someone we know and love. Joseph could interpret dreams and had an unusual insight into God's provision and plan for His people. We may not be able to interpret dreams but we can and should have insight into God's plan. With his own insightfulness, Joseph reminds us of how we too can take those things that have been done, wrongs against us, and see what God did with them to create something good from something that had caused pain.

I think back over my life and can remember moments of hurt, pain, even anguish, from the actions of others. Now I can also see how God has touched my life and the lives of others through some of the events I have suffered. Have I always forgiven others for their transgressions? I have tried. Being magnanimous, like Joseph was to his brothers, takes maturity, understanding, and wisdom. The maturity to patiently wait for the act of someone asking to be forgiven. The understanding to accept an apology when offered. The wisdom to see how God has used the entire affair to make something good happen in someone's life.

Genesis 50:21 "So then, don't be afraid. I will provide for you and your children. And he reassured them and spoke kindly to them."

Forgive. Forget. Fulfill their needs. Joseph can teach us so much about true forgiveness. The same kind of forgiveness that Jesus teaches and uses to grace us with every day. On the cross He begged His Father, "forgive them, for they know not what they do." His suffering puts into place the salvation of the world. Without it there would be no reconciliation between God and man. I am so grateful that He took the sin of the world upon His shoulders, offering forgiveness for any who ask, and in the end, saving the lives of many...

# FORTY-THREE

## Jumping to Conclusions

I had just ordered my lunch when I heard my waitress say to a server in training, "that's what we call a dollar table" as they walked away. Immediately I recognized that she was talking about the fact that I was a single guest, a woman, older, or all three, triple blow, and she expected to get a dollar as a tip for her service. I considered leaving her a note along with her tip, and actually wrote one, tore it up and left her a hefty tip instead. She was a nice young woman and gave good service and I know she never intended for me to hear her words. As a waitress for many years myself, I understood all too well what she meant and I got a great idea for a devotion, so all ended well. How could this be a topic for discussion you ask, well it was in the note I tore up which read, "things are not always as they appear to be."

I knew what that waitress did not, that I had been a server for over twenty years and am personally a strong tipper. Even if I had not overheard her, as long as I received a good service, I would have rewarded it. You see often in life we come to, or jump to, conclusions without all the facts, or at least all the intentions. I remember a time when I came to the conclusion that God did not want me, had no use for someone such as myself as I was too dirty to belong to him, but I was mistaken, he loved me at my most soiled. He loved me even as a broken, miserable piece of woman who was at the lowest point in life; I assumed he could not love me because I did not have all the facts.

When Mary discovered the empty tomb on the Sunday morning after Christ was crucified, she assumed he was stolen since his body was not in the place she expected it to be, things were not as they appeared though. John 20:1-2 "Now on the first day of the week Mary Magdalene came to the tomb early, while it was still dark, and saw that the stone had been taken away from the tomb. So she ran and went to Simon Peter and the other disciple, the one whom Jesus loved, and said to them, "They have taken the Lord out of the tomb, and we do not know where they have laid him." Yes Jesus was no longer in his grave but not because of the reason Mary assumed, but because he was resurrected! It was only a short while before Mary along with the other disciples would see Jesus alive, face to face, but for that brief moment in time she jumped to the conclusion that his body was stolen or simply gone. John 20:15 "Jesus said to her, "Woman, why are you weeping? Whom are you seeking?" Supposing him to be the gardener, she said to him, "Sir, if you have carried him away, tell me where you have laid him, and I will take him away."

We all do this thing, the jumping to conclusions without all the pertinent information to draw from, but when it comes to your salvation there should be no assumptions, know the facts, John 3:3 "Jesus answered him, "Truly, truly, I say to you, unless one is born again he cannot see the kingdom of God." This chapter in John is where you need to seek truth if you think that you have heard the voice of God yet are not quite sure if you have believed on his Son, Jesus Christ. Do not jump to the conclusion that you are saved by knowledge or works, but assume you are not until you have felt the life changing experience of being born again. Do not be fooled by thinking that things are as they appear to be.

All of us find ourselves at some time or another jumping to conclusions without all the information necessary to form an educated decision or we choose our words before we give ourselves time to consider what they mean, and we even assume things about other people without getting to know them and what they are all about. Life is filled with amazing opportunities to discover the truths of what makes other people who they are and why, to discern how much God loves us, and to find in his Word the only way to know your salvation, through knowing Jesus. A little less assumptions and jumping to conclusions, and a lot more seeking real honest answers is called for in all our lives. Remember, things are not always as they appear to be.

# FORTY-FOUR

## Communication

I was having a conversation with a friend the other day and as we talked we both came to a thought at the same time. Just as we desire communication with one another how much more does God long for us to communicate with him who created us for that reason. Consider a moment how it feels as a parent, or child, when there is a long period of silence between you or a friend who you constantly reach out to, yet they don't respond in any way. When we do not pray, when we ignore the very real fact that God is waiting for us to talk to him, we are allowing the distance between us to grow until we begin to feel uncomfortable when we do turn to him. If you have ever had a time in your life when you were separated from someone you loved by silence then you know a little how God must feel when we are silent towards him.

All throughout the Word God's voice can be heard as he spoke to Adam, Noah, Abraham and the prophets; we hear the voice of God in every word spoken by Jesus, and in every beat of our hearts he speaks his truths, his plans, and his love for us if we are but listening. How much more does he want us to reach out to him in prayer, lifting our voices in praise and thanksgiving, even requests for help, hope, and healing express our love for him through a viable form of communication. I believe that God demands nothing less than an open and constant contact with his children.

Psalm 19:3-4,14 "Day to day pours out speech, and night to night reveals knowledge. There is no speech, nor are there words, whose voice is not heard. Let the words of my mouth and the meditation of my heart be acceptable in your sight, O LORD, my rock and my redeemer."

Keeping my eyes on Jesus, my focus on things of my spirit, and an open line of communication with God has changed how I live, how I make decisions, how I love, how I speak to others and how I listen to both them and to God. As I talk with God I have also learned that he has much to tell me as well, if I only open my ears, heart and mind to what he would say. Communication is more, much more than talking, it is having an open and listening ear for what God would have us know. Sometimes it is breathed through the voice of others, sometimes if we listen carefully enough, God speaks directly into our ear. I long to hear the voice of God and I know he not only desires to hear mine, he deserves to hear me speak, listen, and communicate with him every opportunity I have.

# FORTY-FIVE

## Bringing Your Very Best

What do you think God deserves for you to bring as an offering from your life; your very best or just your average gift? Mediocre is not acceptable to God, this I know as throughout all scripture we see the evidence of what is and is not worthy to lay before our King. In the book of Genesis we learn quickly how God feels as Able gives the best and Cain does not. Genesis 4:3-8 "In the course of time Cain brought to the LORD an offering of the fruit of the ground, and Abel also brought of the firstborn of his flock and of their fat portions. And the LORD had regard for Abel and his offering, but for Cain and his offering he had no regard. So Cain was very angry, and his face fell. The LORD said to Cain, "Why are you angry, and why has your face fallen? If you do well, will you not be accepted? And if you do not do well, sin is crouching at the door. Its desire is for you, but you must rule over it." So now we see that from the beginning of creation God has revealed that he demands the best of us, body and soul.

I have come to believe that the best we should be giving to God is more than ten percent tithing, church attendance, and bible reading. The best is giving until we hurt, leading by example in and out of church and having the Word written upon our hearts. The best is doing all we can, giving all of ourselves, and being all we can be to the honor and glory of our Father in Heaven. After all, he gave us the best of himself, time and time again. He gave us his best during creation and you need only look around you at this beautiful earth to see this. He gave his best when breathing his spirit into us as he made us in his own image. He most certainly gave us his best when he became man, sending his only Son to die on the cross for all.

The Word tells us over and over to bring our best, do our best and be our best in order for it to be holy and acceptable to God.

Romans 12:1 "I appeal to you therefore, brothers, by the mercies of God, to present your bodies as a living sacrifice, holy and acceptable to God, which is your spiritual worship."

1 Chronicles 29:9 "Then the people rejoiced because they had given willingly, for with a whole heart they had offered freely to the LORD. David the king also rejoiced greatly."

Colossians 3:23-24 "Whatever you do, work heartily, as for the Lord and not for men, knowing that from the Lord you will receive the inheritance as your reward. You are serving the Lord Christ."

2 Timothy 2:15 "Do your best to present yourself to God as one approved, a worker who has no need to be ashamed, rightly handling the word of truth."

If I am going to present my life as a living sacrifice then I believe it should be with only the best I can give. If I am giving the best I should do so with a joyful heart and doing so freely remembering that it is Jesus Christ I serve. I must be able to respond to the Holy Spirit as he convicts me, approved and unashamed of the calling I am upholding, giving one hundred percent of the best of myself. How we behave towards others, carry ourselves in public, how we dress and even our language, reflects what we are presenting as our best to God, although these may not always be the things that he requires, I think he expects them. I am coming to know, through prayer and meditation, what God expects from me, both physically and spirituality, and I know that he deserves only the best of what I am, what I do, and what I offer as my true sacrifice.

# FORTY-SIX

# Pick Yourself Up

On a recent visit to a fast food restaurant I went to sit down in a chair and somehow managed to either miss the seat or the chair slipped out from under my bottom, whichever, I hit the floor hard, leaving my side and hip badly bruised, along with my ego. After the fall I got up three additional times to retrieve things we needed, and each time that I returned to my chair I carefully made sure that my bottom was in line with the seat and held the chair firmly in my hands to prevent another fall. As I thought more and more about this fall I realized how much this reminds me of my personal walk with the Lord. How often through the years that I made a mistake, taking a fall, only to find myself doing it over and over again. It was hard to fully understand that I was ignoring the fact that I was not holding onto the hand of God, whose hand is the only one that can steady my life and keep me from falling.

We all make mistakes, sin, or simply do not know what the next step is in our journey as we struggle to discern what God would have us do, be, or even who we are becoming. The problem is not with the falling but in the getting up and resetting our lives so that we do not repeat what was the cause of our fall from grace. Much like my careful adjustment of my mindset after missing the chair and hitting the floor, we must be aware of what is needed to not repeat our mistakes that cause our lives to get off track or our fall in the first place. God's plan of mercy and love is filled with forgiveness, grace and redemption, encouraging us to get back up when we fall, learn from how we fell, and not make the same mistake again and again.

As I examined the bruises on my body I realized that they are serving, if only temporarily, to remind me to not only be careful, but to remind me that falling hurts. When we fall from grace it too needs only be temporary and the shame and pain we feel will be wiped away forever as we receive forgiveness and mercy from our Father in Heaven. Any reprimand we may receive will linger only as long as we need, to understand that the pain is for our own good, to make us stronger and more able to go on with our work, our lives, our passion for Christ. We are being refined, we are being made righteous, and should be striving to have the mind of Christ, therefore we know when we fall from grace there is only one thing to do, pick ourselves up and get on with the rest of our lives.

# FORTY-SEVEN

## Selah

Calm down, take a deep breath...Selah, a Hebrew word meaning a musical interlude, used after many psalms, to pause and think about what was. Oh how I can use this in my life, every day, but most particularly when I am beginning to feel just a bit anxious. I can compose my thoughts and think positive, creating a feeling of complete calmness. There are many other times that we can use Selah, to pause and give thanks to God for all he does for us daily, Selah, to stop and consider what the words from my mouth may sound like, Selah, to listen to God's voice in my heart, Selah.

From the psalms I receive such peace and find calm for any trouble; one of my favorites is Psalm 46:1-3 "God is our refuge and strength, a very present help in trouble. Therefore we will not fear though the earth gives way, though the mountains be moved into the heart of the sea, though its waters roar and foam, though the mountains tremble at its swelling. Selah" Stop now, take a breath, think on these verses, and calm down...

There are troubles enough in this life without worrying about tomorrow. Matthew 6:34 "Therefore do not be anxious about tomorrow, for tomorrow will be anxious for itself. Sufficient for the day is its own trouble." Selah I am aware of the positive attitude that overcomes the doubt and fear that comes from the negative thoughts. Battling the anxiety of each challenge, bravely moving forward no matter how hard the situation, takes knowing that God has you covered, as Jesus holds everything together. Colossians 1:17 " And he is before all things, and in him all things hold together." What an amazing thing to know and to keep close to our hearts, that no matter the circumstances, Jesus has it all together, he is in control. Selah

Living a tranquil life in a world growing increasingly chaotic we may often have times when we can see nothing but storms raging, wind howling and waves crashing. These are the moments when our faith in Jesus redefines our attitudes towards the challenges that arise, when we bravely and courageously stand against what would bring us down. Finding our peace and calmness during these storms strengthens us to the point where we know a much deeper and more abiding faith than ever before. Selah

# FORTY-EIGHT

## On Fire

We should be on fire for God, literally, blazing the trails with the fiery power of the Holy Spirit.

1 Peter 1:7 "So that the tested genuineness of your faith-more precious than gold that perishes though it is tested by fire-may be found to result in praise and glory and honor at the revelation of Jesus Christ."

What are we waiting for and why does it seem that many are so quiet today, when we should be shouting the good news of what God has done for us? We should be on fire with the truth, shouting the good news at every opportunity. "Closet Christians", is this what many have become? Afraid of what the world says about us, afraid of what our neighbors think, maybe we are afraid of terrorism; whatever stops us from sharing the gospel I believe it is now time to burst free from these binding chains and throw off the fear and negativity that has become the uniform for the "closet Christian".

We should be putting on the full armor of God, Ephesians 6:11, "Put on the whole armor of God, that you may be able to stand against the schemes of the devil." This then should be the uniform of the Christians on fire as we march into battle to fight the evil forces of satan and offset the damage done by lukewarm "closet Christians". The belt of truth, the breastplate of righteousness, our feet shod with the readiness of the gospel of truth, a shield of faith and helmet of salvation and the sword of the spirit which is the Word of God. This is the uniform of every believer, a soldier in the fight against the world, as we go out to be the voice of Jesus in a world that no longer wants to hear it.

We dear brothers and sisters have a choice to make as disciples of Jesus Christ as it is not only our mission it is our duty, God's command, to not be silent but go bravely forward into the darkness shining the light of the gospel. Proclaiming the Word of God from our mouths and our actions is our testimony, to be silent is to live in fear. 1 John 4:18 "There is no fear in love, but perfect love casts out fear. For fear has to do with punishment, and whoever fears has not been perfected in love."

I am on fire for the Lord and I choose to not be quiet, I will not be a "closet Christian", but boldly accept the responsibility of my discipleship and courageously stand for what I know is truth. I have a voice, I have the full armor of God, and I will stand firm on the solid rock of my life, Jesus Christ.

# FORTY-NINE

# Why Tears?

I am feeling very overwhelmed today, the reason why, because I am being moved by the Holy Spirit like never before in my life. Emotionally speaking I have been on the verge of tears or crying ever since I went to the altar during church services this morning. As I knelt down, I lifted up this coming weekend and the workshop I, and God, have been working on in my heart, for several months. To see the fruition of all the prayers, studying, and writing that I have done on the horizon is filling me with a sense of peace, grace, and gratitude, as I am vividly aware of how God has used me in a powerful and empowering way over the course of preparing for this.

Why tears I ask myself? Why not laughter, or even the giggles as I am overcome with joy and relief at how God has moved in me and moved me to share with those whom he would have me speak to? My heart is pounding, my thoughts are chaotic, and my soul is filled with knowledge, and these things that bring me to my knees serve to bring on a flood of tears as well. I cannot explain why I am so filled with emotion but I do understand why I am, as the Holy Spirit is providing me with strength, courage and a boldness of spirit unlike any I have experienced. I am at peace because of so many who are praying for me, who care about this event that I am working so hard on and as this peace wells up within me its only way out is through my tears.

I have spent countless hours these past months chewing on the subject of fear and anxiety and how God would have me share what I have learned with others. I have spent countless hours praying that God would open my eyes to his truths and write his words upon my heart. A myriad of emotions have raced through my life these past days as the culmination of almost a year spent on this one particular thing is coming to a conclusion. Even though I am assured of my voice, confident in the ability that God has given me, and grateful for the confidence displayed by the ones who ask me to participate, I am motivated only by the Holy Spirit to see this one time ministry concluded.

So now I think of the writing of said emotions, the tears still falling, and I am so grateful for the gift of sharing. I am amazed at how moved emotionally I am today but I am enthralled by the power of the Holy Spirit moving in me every day. As you read this now, I hope that you too will be moved, moved to take a moment out of your time and lift me up to our Father. Pray that I will truly use the few days left to listen to his voice, as he quiets my pounding heart, fills me with the peace that surpasses all understanding and that as promised, he would keep my tears in a bottle.

# FIFTY

# A Positive Attitude

Turn your negatives into positives... I am finding as I grow older and mature in my journey through this life that no matter the circumstances, big or small, high level worry or low level anxiety, the positive attitude overcomes the negative. The impact on worry or doubt is fed through the negative emotions that we have making things seem worse than they most likely are. The positive attitude overcomes the worry and fear, freeing us to move bravely forward with what we have to face, challenges all. I am grateful that God, through the Holy Spirit, has revealed this to me as I have so often in my past allowed negativity to dictate how I dealt with ordinary and extraordinary problems.

Negativity feeds fear while positivity fuels faith. I am discovering more and more the power of positive thinking when it comes to faith and how it continues to grow with every new challenge I face. Similar to "finding the silver lining", the happy, optimistic thoughts lift our spirits and produces an abiding faith that grows as we continue to believe in the power of God and allow ourselves and our thoughts to be guided by him. Picture that dark cloud hanging over your head as negativity and as it serves to dampen your thoughts it also eventually turns doubt and anxiety into fear. We need to choose which scenario we want for ourselves, the one that creates less havoc and chaos in our lives, or the one that in all certainty leads to depression and anxiety.

Philippians 4:13 "I can do all things through him who strengthens me."

This, beloved, is Christ, from whom we get the power to choose the positive attitude in every area of our lives; through Christ who has provided for us a stronghold to lean on in times of trouble and crisis, when fear threatens us, we have a rock to stand fearlessly and boldly upon. Keep your eyes focused on Jesus, do not look away from his light, and you will find the courage to overcome doubt, anxiety, and fear. The negatives (fears) will still come but will have no power over you as you take the hand of Christ and allow him to guide you through your most frightening storms.

One final thought about the negative and positive attitude in our lives. Remember that when your mind focuses on the negative you are at your most vulnerable to have satan do his best to keep you in that negative state. He will use everything within his power to do so, the media, your negative memories, and your doubts about the future are all fuel to keep your fears in his control, not your own. But when you stay focused on the positive you keep control, allowing the Holy Spirit to speak to you, reminding you of your hope, faith, and joy, and all the things that God has brought you through, these will strengthen your courage so that you will boldly face any fears that come your way.

# FIFTY-ONE

## Blank Pages

We all start life with a blank page and it is up to ourselves whether it is filled with flowing script or ineligible scribbles. Sometimes we have to erase a mistake or two, but that only serves to give us room to add more of the beautiful calligraphy that represents the amazing and often mysterious message that is our life. What do the pages of our lives tell about us? They describe our innermost thoughts and feelings, revealing our true nature. As we age our pages build one upon another until finally they become a book, a glorious saga of all the days, good and bad that have filled the years we have lived.

What type of book will be written from the pages of your life? Will it be one of adventure and excitement, a mystery? Maybe it is filled with one romantic story after another, a true romance novel. It could be a family friendly book with chapter after chapter of uplifting and easygoing tales. Whatever you are writing, one thing is for sure that at some time or another it will have "the end" written on the last page and where it ends here in this life, it will amazingly pick up once more, sometime in the future.

I love the analogy of our lives being blank pages waiting for us to fill up with our own personal experiences, our stories captured forever in time. Of course this thought, our lives being the pages we write our life stories upon, is not new by any stretch of the imagination and yet the writing of such stuff feels eloquent and fires my pen to paper to put into words how I hope my own blank pages have been filled and how they continue.

At the end of my life will it read as a wholesome family saga, an extremely adventurous tale, or will it be a spiritual prose filled with amazing and graceful twists and turns? I believe that my pages, like most people's, will be some of all of this, and I am wise enough, I think, to make sure it is thus as I have control over my actions and reactions to everything I face. What was once a blank page is now page after page of lovely text, pictures drawn from and written out by my own experiences.

# FIFTY-TWO

## Motivation

Motivation; what gets us moving and what exactly keeps us moving? Is there a carrot dangling at the end of a string while we go faster and faster trying to catch that prize? There may not be an actual carrot dangling in front of us but there is almost certainly always a reward for our actions and thus we are motivated to move, keep moving, and do the best in every situation, in every job that we take on for ourselves. The prize is most often money, paycheck, payment for services rendered, the typically expected reward. Or, it can be an all together different motivator, life itself.

Life and its glorious gifts: the beauty of the earth and its seasons, the love we feel one for another, the first cry of a newborn baby, the endlessly rewards of every day, blessings upon blessings heaped upon us, the children of God. The motivation is all around us to live life to the fullest, you must open your eyes and ears to know it, if you do you will see it everywhere. Life is the prize that dangles like a carrot in front of us; but we must be motivated by something more than normal life in order to ensure that we continue to seek the very best it offers in reward for a well lived and full life.

There is a reward unequaled by any other in the pursuit of happiness in this world and that is everlasting life that is the eternal reward when you believe on Jesus Christ as your personal savior. What motivates you and I to actively seek this gift, as it is not something earned, but freely given, available for everyone? I can only tell you what motivates me, and that is the spirit filled, deeply emotional impact of joy that is indescribable and holds more promise than gold or riches, and merits no understanding as it is undeserved and unexpected with every new morning. That is the only motivation I need.

Now, what motivates me to share all of this? The greatest of all motivators, love. The carrot dangling at the end of the stick should be the realization that by sharing the truth of God's plan for us all, that those who do not know will hear and believe, will see and know that there is no other way. And that in the seeing and the hearing, in the believing and the knowing, they too will be rewarded with the joy and peace that comes from God. It is a wonderful cycle of motivation, I am motivated to motivate you.

# FIFTY-THREE

## Loneliness

There are those who are alone every day, day in and day out; maybe they are not able to go out due to a disability or disease, or they are retired, widowed, and alone. Some people are alone by choice, desiring to be by themselves instead of having to deal with others; these hermit like individuals are most likely not lonely. But many people are alone by circumstances, not by desire. What can we do to meet this great enemy, loneliness, that strikes thousands of people every day? First, we have to recognize that they are indeed alone and that they do not want to be that way. If we turn our hearts and heads away from the lonely, pretending that we cannot or do not see them, we do ourselves an injustice and them an even greater one.

What does the Word say about loneliness and our role and God's in the issues surrounding this profound problem?

Genesis 2:18 "Then the LORD God said, "It is not good that the man should be alone; I will make him a helper fit for him." It is not good for man to be alone; from the beginning of time God's intention was for us not to be alone, so much so that his first act after creating a man was giving him a woman to keep him company and be his helpmate. God created us, you and I in order to have communion with him as our Father and with one another, of course he does not want us to be alone, and for this profound reason it is so very important that we are aware of those who may be alone and lonely.

Psalms 25:16 "Turn to me and be gracious to me, for I am lonely and afflicted." The psalmist writes poetically of loneliness as an affliction, like a disease and is asking for graciousness to be shown on him. I wonder how long he suffered before he asked for help? I wonder if we have people in our own lives who do not ask for help with their loneliness? We must become focused on more than our own busy lives to see if there are lonely people who would give anything to have their affliction eased.

Hebrews 13:1-2 "Let brotherly love continue. Do not neglect to show hospitality to strangers, for thereby some have entertained angels unawares." Although this scripture does not directly speak about loneliness I felt led to add it as we should remember that as brothers and sisters in Christ Jesus we should never forget what we have been taught by him and through his disciples within the Word of the New Testament. If we see a need that we know we can meet for someone, then I believe we should not miss out on the opportunity to do something. Loneliness fits into the mold of hospitality in today's world as we can offer ourselves as company to shut-ins, the elderly, disabled, and the sick, meeting a need that they may have not had the courage to ask for help or known anyone who could help alleviate their loneliness.

Are you lonely, or do you suffer from chronic loneliness? Even though it seems sarcasm to write this, you are not alone. Many people are in similar situations and you can take heart in the idea that there are many who do care about your loneliness. There may come a time to do what is necessary to alleviate your own loneliness. Reach out to a loved one, church, or friend, sharing your needs with someone who can help you overcome the loneliness by visiting with you, taking you out, or even through a phone call. We are called to love our neighbors as ourselves, second only to loving God; if you reach out in loneliness to someone who does not respond then "shake the dust off your sandals" and move on to another brother or sister. If you for even a moment can get relief from your loneliness, then think how much better your life will become.

Healing for the sick, the poor at heart and the lonely is ours to claim. Psalm 147:3 "He heals the brokenhearted and binds up their wounds." I pray that we will open our hearts and eyes to those who are lonely, who may be desperately in need of companionship and love...

# FIFTY-FOUR

## The Cookie Jar

How do you celebrate Valentine's day or do you even celebrate at all? It is typically thought (by men) that it is a holiday drummed up by the greeting card companies to increase sales of cards, and this is most likely true. If you think about it that is the reason for most of the push towards advertising the celebration of all our major holidays, to make money. But still, I like the idea of flowers and candy, dinner for two and all the romance flowing on February fourteenth; it is simply the sweetest day. Do I need all the romance, flowers, and candy, no, actually I do not. As it happens, my husband is not exactly a romantic, but what he lacks in romance he more than makes up with love, gratitude, and attitude. I have come to realize that love is an attitude. The feeling of love is an emotion, the act of love is a verb, but the essence of love is attitude.

The definition of attitude: a settled way of thinking or feeling about something or someone, typically one that is expressed in one's behavior. There are obviously many ways to express our attitude of love for each other, whether it is a romantic relationship, a blood relationship, or a spiritual relationship; each one offering its own unique style of expression. Romantic love is shared between a man and a woman who are drawn together for two reasons, physical attraction and spiritual similarities. Love shared between two or more people due to their beliefs is a spiritual love. Finally we have the connecting love between family, brothers and sisters who share their past through memories, their present by keeping close, and their future through their children and grandchildren. Loving relationships have long lived attitudes of peace, understanding, and faithfulness; even more so I think they are filled with an awareness of each other's hearts and desires.

That brings me to the cookie jar. An old cracked container that although not an antique it was a piece that was a beautiful memory from our mother's kitchen. The cookie jar was given to my sister years ago by our mother because she had always said she would like to have it for her own. It sat on my sister's kitchen counter for years until just a short while ago, when with her own generous nature she gave it in a show of friendship to her new neighbor. They had just gotten to know one another when her friend noticed the cookie jar and excitedly exclaimed that her mother had had one just like it and so after thoughtful consideration, my sister gave away her favorite memory piece. Unfortunately the friendship between the two did not last and this part of the story I will omit, only to say that my sister's generosity was something she did not regret.

A few weeks ago while shopping at a local antique shop, I ran across an identical cookie jar and excitedly discovered the price was more than affordable so I purchased it for my sister. Although it was the same cookie jar, instead of being cracked, it was stained. I almost hesitated giving it to her, but after praying and thinking on it, decided it would make a special birthday gift. My sister agreed. She was so happy to have another cookie jar, and although she and I both know it is not the very same one our mother had used, it now held an even deeper meaning and message of love between two sisters. A friend that my sister told the story to just the other day expressed it this way, "Now that's love!" She could have said, "Now that's a great attitude!"

Love is a deep expression of our attitudes towards each other and no where do we find that expressed in any greater way then through the love of Jesus for each of us. His love was an attitude that was a beautiful expression of physical, emotional, and spiritual love, even a touch romantic too. Through physical love God made himself flesh to sacrifice his life on the cross, through emotional love we read in scripture Jesus cried out to God for forgiveness for us even while on the cross, through spiritual love he gave us the Holy Spirit, and through romantic love in that God prepared before creation the story that was always written for the sacrifice of his only Son, which was the only way to show his abiding love for his children.

A simple cookie jar, a sister's love, a husband's attitude whether romantic or just loving, and a Savior's sacrifice, these are the best things to think about on Valentine's Day. An opportunity arises to celebrate love of every degree, show appreciation through a card, flowers, candy, or invent a beautiful new way to express your love, but never forget that love is not merely a verb, an action, it is an attitude...

# FIFTY-FIVE

## Forbidden Fruit

While enjoying some delicious tangerines at breakfast this morning, okay they were "cuties", the idea of which fruit was the fruit from the Tree of Knowledge in the garden of Eden came to mind. Was it that elusive apple, or maybe the exotic pomegranate? Was it a peach, a pear, or a banana? Does it matter, no, does it make for an interesting discussion, we will see. What was really going on in that garden that we need to understand? Is it really all about the fruit? Could it not just as easily have been an almond tree or another delicious and hard to pass on food? All through the Bible we find the use of trees in parables, in prophecy, and in prayers, the Tree of Knowledge is only the beginning, just as Eve's sin was only the start, no matter the fruit that God chose to grow on that particular tree.

It is more about the characters than the props, it is more about the discussion than the fruit, and more about the knowledge than the Tree. As I bit into the juicy sweet tangerines I could only imagine what was so tempting that caused Eve to throw complete caution to the wind. I don't think it was the fruit that tempted her at all but the thrill of the sin and the act of defiance. "Here," she said to her partner, Adam, "try it you'll like it!" Hold up there, did I just say she offered some to Adam? So, he was there all along? I don't know about you (women) but I believe I sense something odd about that defiant woman being allowed by her man to take this great leap into sin with nary a word being spoken except by the snake. What does the scripture say about this? Genesis 2:16-17 "And the LORD God commanded the man, saying, "You may surely eat of every tree of the garden, but of the tree of the knowledge of good and evil you shall not eat, for in the day that you eat of it you shall surely die." So Adam knew, he had been fairly warned about the consequences, yet he stood by and listened in on his wife, Eve, talking to that old devil and watched as she reached for the orange, apple or pear, and took a bite. Just like that the act was done, and then, yes then, he took and ate. Genesis 3:6-7 "So when the woman saw that the tree was good for food, and that it was a delight to the eyes, and that the tree was to be desired to make one wise, she took of its fruit and ate, and she also gave some to her husband who was with her, and he ate. Then the eyes of both were opened, and they knew that they were naked. And they sewed fig leaves together and made themselves loincloths."

Open the eyes of my heart Lord is a prayer I often say, sometimes several times a day. Here we find a situation where God has spoken a command to his children, the very first of his creation, and they ignored it so as to have their eyes opened, so to speak. They didn't pray for the eyes of their hearts to be opened, but disobedient, they sought to have open the eyes of their minds, their very souls, and for the first time in our history, a sin was carried out. What kind of fruit trees? Was it moist, juicy, and sweet? That is not what matters here, what is important is that God has given us commands, he has given us the choice to obey or not, and he has clearly demonstrated the cost of what that forbidden fruit has attached to it, death. We have determined that Adam stood, seemingly casually, by, watching as his wife brought sin into the world and there is a great lesson here for us all. Most important, being obedience, but add to that, not standing idly by and watch while your spouse, child, sister or brother, anyone at all, commits sin when you know that it is a sin they are about to commit. Reach out, grab that tangerine from their hands and say, "Now you know better than that and if you don't, let me help you see the light", then pray with them, "Open the eyes of our hearts Lord."

# FIFTY-SIX

## Valentine's Cards

I saw a picture of old fashioned Valentine's day cards the other day and was amazed at how big they were. It seems when I was in elementary school the cards were much bigger than those made today for kids to share. So many things have changed throughout the span of my life, technology, travel, education, clothes, diets, and yes Valentine cards. Not all change is good and certainly all change is not bad, but there are times that I often wish that certain things would stay the same forever. An example, my grandchildren, who are growing up far too quickly and seem to change with every new day, which make me long to hold time in place if even for a little while. Of course my wishful thinking will not make it happen, but still I am sorry for some of the changes in the world and in my life over the years, yet I embrace many of them as well.

For instance, take the telephone, the evolution of said device is something extraordinary. From a huge box on the wall, to the rotary dial, to the large bulky original cellular phones to today's sleek thin I phone, the instrument of a hundred generations (exaggerated) is a change that I am not complaining about, as I am sure we all can agree. Cars, appliances, music, styles, and television(s) are on the list of good change, but what about those changes I am not so happy about. Christmas; I loved the old fashioned way of celebrating Christmas when it was time, and not weeks before and with all the materialism of today. School; I remember when the teacher had authority to teach with discipline and parents were not afraid to send their children there. The media; I appreciated the news and entertainment industry when they told it like it was, not like today when they use a story to gain earnings and ratings, telling people not what is always true but what the media wants them to believe.

Now on to something and someone who has never changed and never will do so. God. God the Father, God the Son, and God the Holy Spirit; these three have always been with us, always together since the creation of the world. Genesis 1:26 "Then God said, "Let us make mankind in our image, in our likeness, so that they may rule over the fish in the sea and the birds in the sky, over the livestock and all the wild animals, and over all the creatures that move along the ground." God speaking clearly here that even before the creation he was not alone as he was in the company of Jesus and the Holy Spirit. Our unchanging God, the unchanged trinity, the certain and unchanging plan that was set in motion by God's own divine hand with the promise that he is the same, yesterday, today and always. Hebrews 13:8 "Jesus Christ is the same yesterday and today and forever." I am so grateful for this as in a world where there is continuing change, when it seems nothing ever stays the same, we can rely and trust in our unchanging God.

# FIFTY-SEVEN

## The Entire Package

Have you ever been a part of a bake sale where you purchase and bake the ingredients, wrap and price the finished product, set up displays and work the event, only to buy back some of the items that you provided in the first place? If you have, you know that it's an amazing experience. Our church this past weekend had a book and bake sale, it went amazingly well, and brought to mind this idea of giving back the entire package that has been given to us.

All that we have, all that we are, comes, beginning to end, from God. As we belong to him who has so graciously provided us with everything we could possibly need, we are endowed with the responsibility to be good and generous stewards of what have.  Since we understand and believe that it all comes from our Father in Heaven we then must realize that in the giving back to him, it may be expected of us to give much more than a pittance that we drop in the plate on Sunday morning. Sometimes he wants it all, that which we received with an open heart, used for his greater good, for our own needs, and returned back from where it came with an open heart and mind.

In a novel I read once there was a story line in which a woman in the mid nineteenth century wanted to see her small town have a "subscription" library. After various festivals, parties and fund raising events, it became a reality. One line I particularly remember from the book, "And after all Anne had done to help make the library a success, she proudly bore home her first book checked out in her own name." I want to be more like this woman, Anne. I want to work hard at every task, every opportunity, that God calls me to, and give until I have given all that he demands of me, and proudly and joyfully take home the knowledge that I did all I could.

It is the entire package that God expects us to give. Whether it is time, money, intellect, physical prowess, spiritual assistance, or all of these, when called upon to give we must be ready, if asked, to bring our all, from the beginning to the end, the entire package must be placed at the altar. Buy the ingredients, bake the brownies, wrap them in plastic wrap, sell them to yourself, and proudly bear the results of a job well done for God, giving the entire package. I learned a beautiful lesson from a small group of God's people who were willing to do just that this past weekend.

FIFTY-EIGHT

The Gardens

In England and probably the entire British Isles, they refer to their yard as a garden, while in America of course a garden is a place where we grow vegetables and flowers, but not grass. I think though, that it is quite a lovely idea to say my yard is a garden as it conjures up images of lush box wood hedges dotted with tiny flowers, primroses, miniature dogwood trees, and cobblestone pathways winding up and down all throughout. In reality it is still just a yard, but the isn't it strange that the simple change of a name can make the mundane seem extraordinary?

There is something else that I'm reminded of when I think of a garden, the garden of Gethsemane, where Jesus spent his last night on this earth. Instead of images of fauna and flora, there are thoughts of bended knees, uplifted face, folded hands and sweat pouring off his face in the form of blood. In place of cobblestone pathways I see trampled grass, boot and sandal marks from both soldiers and disciples. And I see in place of the peace and quiet of an English garden, the struggle between good and evil, God and satan. I walk through my garden seeking a reward, of sight, taste and smell; Christ experienced a garden of sacrifice, redemption and love.

A garden, whether a place of peace, or a place of sacrifice, a bounty of fruits and vegetables or a harvest of redeeming grace displayed for a dark world to grasp, it is an ideal that has changed my heart and spirit. I picture myself walking through a beautiful place, filled with lovely things to see, love to be consumed, and redemption at every twist and turn. I also see my Lord and Savior, Jesus, walking beside me. Now I can imagine my garden as a true combination of the Garden of Gethsemane and the Garden of Eden; what was and what was meant to be. As I walk through the garden of my life my spirit is filled with joy as I know that I will never again allow any weeds to grow here, nor darkness to enter.

# FIFTY-NINE

## Temptations

My husband and I are on a diet, an everlasting, non-stop, healthy lifestyle and drop a few pounds diet. That's why it's crazy that when you look in my kitchen cabinets and refrigerator you will find: donuts, cookies, candy, snack cakes, chips, crackers, three different breads, and well you get the picture...Yet, you will also find fresh fruits and veggies, bottles of water, fat free yogurt, lean meats...again, you get the picture. As I was gathering ingredients for making baked goods for our church book and bake sale this weekend I realized the significance of all this to my diet and it is simply, why do we put such temptation in our way? Why do we even bring these splurge foods into our house? I know why; it is that shopping while so hungry and buying everything that I can get my hands on syndrome that fills my kitchen with all kinds of yummy temptations.

This can be similar to how we live spiritually. I know what tempts me, I have an imaginary list for things that I should not do, how I should not act, or be. I have another list of what I should be doing, how I should act and be. Much like the choices in my refrigerator and food pantry that dictate my diet, I have choices from my spiritual lists that control everything I do, whether it is good or bad. I may not always choose from a list of sins like my grocery list, but I am aware of what is lying around, at home, work, or socially that tempts me. I am fully culpable for choosing a spiritual diet of sinful choices or a diet that is rich in God's word, his will, and the joy that comes with living within the boundaries of my imaginary "good choices list." Just as eating healthy and not food shopping while hungry will determine what I bring into my home to eat, making good, healthy choices from praying and studying God's word will keep the good choices front and center of my spiritual diet.

# SIXTY

## Questions

"What plans do you have today?" My husband posed this question to me this morning and I responded, "Nothing much." And then my calendar alarm on my phone went off, and as they say, the rest is history...an appointment for our dog's bath, two orders to enter and a quote to put out for work, reorganization of our laundry room and washing of laundry, several phone calls to make, filing (ugh) and that was just for today. Clean the guest room, oil change, lunch date, bible study, book and bake sale, family weekend, and food shopping for afore mentioned family weekend and bake sale, that rounds off the week, not to mention everyday life, cleaning, work, writing, and errands. Sheweeee, I don't think I'll ever respond to "what plans do you have today" with "nothing much" again.

"Can you come here a minute?" Another trick question isn't it? What constitutes a minute? Is it a clock minute, sixty seconds of time? Or is it a slang for "however long I need you"? Is it a trap? In my house I think it's a mix of trap and however long I need you. Honestly, why do I always fall for that innocently asked question? I can answer that easily, because he (my husband) needs me, and I love being needed. I admit that sometimes it's my imagination that the "minute" is more than sixty seconds, due to the nature of the request. For instance, if the need includes anything to do with climbing a ladder, that minute turns into eternity, or if it means I have to stand in one position holding something steady, it turns into an hour....but if it is almost anything else I honestly do enjoy (for the most part) spending that "minute" of time with my husband.

Where is my.....wait...I don't know, I haven't seen it...I didn't have it last...another loaded question, so beware, because if you even hesitate as if you are going to respond you are in big trouble. I am not against assisting someone (husband) when they (or someone else) have lost something but I know better than to mislead them into having a glimmer of hope that I may know where the lost item is, or horror, I used it last and put it somewhere different than where it goes (not that I ever do that). There is one place in our home, no make that two places, where we find ourselves in the most troubling situations of loss (misplaced) items, the kitchen and our office. For years my husband ran the office alone, until I came on board with my entirely different set of organizational skills, enough said, and the other is the kitchen, again, enough said.

There are many questions in life that are unanswerable, and some questions, as with the above three, that are not only unanswerable, but the responses may be better left unspoken or at the least, not said out loud before a bit of pondering first. In my vast, laughable, experience, sometimes it's just better if you keep your plans to yourself, don't offer your time, and don't ever know where something missing may be hidden. But, if you follow this advice, you may find yourself alone, with a lot of time on your hands, never finding the remote control again....

# SIXTY-ONE

## Attention

Sitting here on a lazy Sunday afternoon and I see on my coffee table a withering, dried up bouquet of flowers which needs to be thrown out and gives me reason to look around my home and check all my plants. I have several of these but there is one in particular that requires special attention all the time, a fern. It is much more sensitive than the other plants I have, needing more water, more sun, and cleaning up around them as their leaves are constantly falling onto my carpet. I really don't mind this, as I love my plants, all of them, and realize that each one has its own special needs for me to not only meet but to appreciate as well. I actually spend more time with the fern as it beckons me with its cry for attention with every dry leaf that falls.

This is so much like our relationship with our Father in Heaven; as we become increasingly aware of his love and care for each of us we can see how he meets our individual needs at the same time. I have to admit, at times I am awful hard to take care of. Sometimes I am more like my fern than my cactus. I go all dry and my leaves start to fall off, no not literally, but spiritually, and I need desperately to go to the well (God's Word) and drink with thirst until I am once again drenched in his love for me. I am grateful for his never-ending love and concern for his children, even as we are all different, we all need his quenching living water more at sometimes than others. Too, just as I clean up after my fern, I believe God comes and helps me clean up any of the messes I make in life.

So I have just written an analogy between the Christian and a houseplant, but it is not yet done. I see how each of my plants are beautiful, thriving under my care, and serve to clean the air I breathe and bring beauty into my home. They tell me their needs by yellowing leaves that eventually turn brown due to too much water or too little. They occasionally bloom, or unexpectedly have a growth spurt with fresh green shoots, and I can see that with my loving care they are thriving. It is really just the same with my relationship with God, as he knows my needs, but he sometimes waits for me to examine myself, my heart, and my spirit, reaching out to him for support and that all encompassing love that he is offering to pour over me. I am thriving, growing, and blooming under his care and I hope just as my plants bring beauty and happiness into my world, I am bringing beauty and happiness into God's world.

# SIXTY-TWO

## My Grandmother's Hands

My grandmother's hands...I glimpsed my hand today and had one of those de ja vu moments; whose hand was I looking at, mine or someone else's? There was a certain something about my it, the fullness of it, the age spot on its surface. It was for but a fleeting moment, but it was not my hand, but my grandmother's. The soft wrinkles and lines, not as harsh as I remembered hers to be but the shape and the coloring were the same.

My grandmother's hands; work worn, calloused, scarred, yet gently loving and soft. Memories came flooding back of her stirring something on her stove, carrying a water bucket into the kitchen through the back door, and scrubbing clothes on an old washboard. Along with those thoughts I remember those hands touching my heart as she did her best to teach me how to cook, pulled a brush through my hair to put it in its rubber band ponytail, and lifted a saucer of coffee to her mouth poured from the cup to cool faster.

My grandmother's hands; mine may not have seen the hard work and difficult situations like hers did, but the shape is there, the aging and creases from time and use, and how they have served me well, as hers did. And today they have blessed me by bringing this rush of memories; my determined and selfless grandmother, and her aging but ageless hands. Those precious hands taught me, loved me, touched me and I am grateful that my hands remind me of my grandmother's.

# SIXTY-THREE

## Cutting Away

This morning as I was getting a cup of coffee I looked up and glanced out the window to see a tree where huge limbs had been cut away, yet the tree had continued to grow taller and stronger. The cutting off of dead and useless limbs had evidently caused a growth spurt that was necessary to the tree's health and well being. God spoke to me in that moment, saying that I too needed to cut away some things that were hurting me and had actually turned to sin. This is called pruning and as a dear friend reminded me when I confided in her, God is not finished with us, as we are works in progress, and thank God he never will be finished, so my prayer is that he will always convict me and show me what I need to change in order to continue growing.

I considered what exactly I may need to get rid of at this particular moment that was holding me back from growing and producing fruit. Today it was jealousy; yes jealousy had reared its ugly head and shame filled me to the depths of my soul. What, you may ask, would cause such jealousy that God convicted me of it? It was envy from seeing someone else's work, writing, shared on Facebook. Yes, as I saw the post in my feed, I became instantly envious and so very bitter. Of course it passed quickly, but I knew what I had felt, and more importantly God knew.

Jealousy, even a fleeting moment of envy, is unacceptable to God and can only create bitterness for the one who experiences this emotion. I discovered today that it is not an emotion that I want to feel, ever, and I am grateful for this and for my Father who loves me enough to convict me of my sin, forgive me of it, and show me how to take the situation and use it for a lesson that causes spiritual growth in my life...

# SIXTY-FOUR

# The Words of Jesus

The words, or voice, of Jesus has become my heart's ministry since the beginning of the new year. I have been convicted by the Holy Spirit to be all about service and I can see no better place to seek a plan for this than from God himself revealed through the scriptures, the voice of Jesus. Already I have written several pieces, devotions and posts, that have come directly from Jesus' sermons, using one in particular, The Sermon on the Mount. The voice of Jesus has created in me a desire to see myself stand firmly planted on my own mountain, from where my writing can share all of the wonderful and powerful thoughts and truths that God is giving to me.

All through the Word we can hear the voice of Jesus and as I listen to what it says to me I can see the change it is invoking in my life, my writing and in my spiritual walk. Matthew 5:48 "You therefore must be perfect, as your heavenly Father is perfect." There is something spectacularly challenging and rewarding in the knowledge that I can be perfect; Christ says not only should I be but that I must be. As obedience is playing out in my entire ministry and I am adding service to my journey, perfection is certainly what I must strive for, ultimately claiming perfection because it is what the Lord not only expects, demands of me.

"Do not lay up for yourselves treasures on earth, where moth and rust destroy and where thieves break in and steal, but lay up for yourselves treasures in heaven, where neither moth nor rust destroys and where thieves do not break in and steal. For where your treasure is, there your heart will be also." Matthew 6:19-21 I want to know that I have lived such a life that my treasure is not evident anywhere except within my heart. I want to be an example of what we can achieve and set aside as real treasure such as that which Christ is promising will be awaiting us in heaven by my appreciation and devotion to the gift that my God has given me, my life. It matters little what I achieve in this life if it is measured by material things, but I will have accomplished great things if they are counted by heaven's measure.

The words of Jesus echo through the ages, unchanging and unchangeable as they stand as the voice of God. Come with me on this journey in the months ahead as I study, learn, and use the scriptures to reveal what he, Jesus, wants us to know, to understand, and to share. As I travel through the Word I am excited to see the heights that my ministry of writing can reach, the glorious revelations that will be revealed, and the voice of God speaking clearly to me through the words of Jesus.

# SIXTY-FIVE

## Traveling

A year of traveling, yes, I was on the road a lot of last year, work trips, family trips, and combinations of both trips. Looking at the word "trip", I am reminded not so much of traveling today but of falling down, the action of being tripped up by life, by sin, by disobedience, and by Satan. It happens to us all at one time or another, sometimes there is a series of events that lead up to a tripping point, a chain reaction so to speak, and we may get caught up in our actions (sins) and cannot always pull ourselves out before we fall.

Fallen but not forever, out of grace, but not mercy; and there is such an amazing example to follow when we are tempted to sin, when the voice of Satan seems to overshadow the voice of God. In Matthew we read the story of Jesus and the time spent in the desert being tempted by the evil one after spending forty days without food because he was fasting. Three times Satan tempted Jesus to use his power as God to do things that he would not, refused to do and in his own words gave us the power to fight off temptation but also the realization that if we trip and fall, he, Jesus Christ, our God, understands that temptation.

Read that scripture over and over and receive the grace, strength, and power to overcome Satan when he puts temptation in your way, and even if you find yourself succumbing to the temptation and trip and even fall, the words of Jesus will encourage and empower you to pick yourself up, ask for forgiveness and move forward. Remember his responses: "Man shall not live by bread alone, but on every word that comes from the mouth of God, It is also written, do not put your God to the test, and Away from me Satan, for it is written, worship the Lord your God, and serve only him." Christ in his own temptation gives us the very key to understanding how to live in such a way we never again fall, maybe we stumble or trip, but we will not succumb to temptation and fall.

I look forward to traveling in the coming year, work, family, and hopefully some trips for my ministry; what I pray does not happen is a "trip" that causes me to stumble and fall in my spiritual life. With the words of Jesus reverberating in my mind, heart and spirit, I know that I will have the power to fight off temptation and stay on course with the plans God has for my life, this year and beyond.

# SIXTY-SIX

## Gifts

Lots of useful, thoughtful, and even whimsical gifts were given and received this Christmas; I know because I was the recipient of a one that was some sort of each of these things. I was truly blessed with more than my share of presents to unwrap and enjoy and more than one of those was whimsical. As a matter of fact I used one of those gifts today and thus was born this devotion. My son gave me a gift that was not only useful and thoughtful, it was whimsical; a UV light nail dryer.

Now that may seem a strange gift and even stranger that it birthed a devotion but it really is not that at all but extraordinary and hopeful. Extraordinary because the gift was given simply because of a sacrifice that I had made months ago and hopeful because that sacrifice has not been forgotten, in fact it has created a new and powerful impulse in the life of someone very dear to me. This is a wonderful testament to human nature and the spirit's desire to champion what is good and worthy, what someone conceived to be a genuine effort on my part to give up something I enjoyed in order to support a new missionary family.

So let me continue by saying this gift was useful because it is a tool in my everyday life, an assistant of sorts, it is thoughtful for the reason of what a time saver it will be and whimsical because the product itself belongs in a salon not one's home, yet it has appeared in mine. The story behind this gift is simple; I gave up having professional manicures to save money because I wanted to add another missionary family to our giving list and my husband and I decided to ensure that we could afford to do this that I would have to give something up.

I have missed getting my nails done solely because I miss the precious woman who was my chosen technician, and who was most understanding when I explained I was no longer going to be coming to her. I do not have any problems at all doing my own manicure with the exception of getting them to dry before taking on a chore; being at home often causes that to happen. This is where the thoughtful gift came in as my husband realized how often I had to redo a nail or nails because of smears. He suggested the gift to my son.

The gift and story behind it, is one of true commitment and recognition of such and has served to remind me of God's command to let our light shine before men. Matthew 5:16 "In the same way let your light shine before others, that they may see your good deeds and glorify your Father in Heaven." As my husband has shared my sacrifice with my son, he in turn is coming into his own understanding of true commitment and sacrifice to God and the reward of such action. In telling this story today I hope to shine some light for you on your own personal sacrifice and whether or not you would share does not matter, because you and God know the truth and he will remember your sacrifice.

Useful, thoughtful, whimsical; a gift that has touched my heart and serves to remind me of God's promise to remember my sacrifice, has served to show me that my husband still appreciates what I have given up, and also serves to encourage my son to see the worth in not only sacrifice but in the action of giving in its sincerity and entirety. A simple story of a Christmas gift and of simple sacrifice, yet the echoes of love will continue on long after the gift has been forgotten.

# SIXTY-SEVEN

# The Day After Christmas

The morning after Christmas and there is an especially good feeling deep inside the hearts of men and women due to the expected arrival of salvation just the day before. For weeks the world has been preparing to celebrate this momentous occasion, anxiously awaiting the Christmas child, the baby Jesus born to bring the gift of eternal life. Is this really an accurate picture of the last month or so, or is it an image that this writer would draw out of her own imagination?

How many people really awaited with longing hearts the arrival of Christmas for the spiritual blessings received or were they more excited for the material gifts handed out all around. Is it too farfetched to think that Christ really was a huge part of Christmas? My family and friends gathered together, we shared meals and exchanged gifts and there were occasions that the name of Jesus was never mentioned, yet, we knew he was there, we held him close within our hearts and our spirits felt his worth through the Holy Spirit dwelling in us and the light shining out of us. We prepared our hearts and received the greatest gift of all, the Holy Spirit dwelling in us and the constant presence of God.

I hope that you felt that all encompassing love that the Holy Spirit was offering to wrap you up in on Christmas day and will continue to draw strength, joy, peace, and love from it all the year long, for all your life. My prayer is that this will be the year that the glowing warmth of Jesus, through the celebration of his birth, will not only linger, but grow in intensity, spreading from person to person, heart to heart. As we rush to go about taking down the decorations, taking back the unwanted gifts, and throwing out the leftover meals, I pray we will not be too quick to let go of the Christmas Spirit, the love that came down to bring eternal life for me and you...

# SIXTY-EIGHT

## Less is More

I am baking less cookies this Christmas, doing less shopping and wrapping too. We cut back on the decorations both inside and out, less lights, ribbons, greenery, and much less electricity used. We did not receive as many Christmas cards, a shame, because I want our post office to stay busy, but nevertheless there were not as many packages delivered or rings of our doorbell with odd shaped boxes to put away. We stopped spending until it hurt, yet have given much more of ourselves, which actually felt so much better. We tried to make this year's celebration more about others than ourselves, and the cutting back on everything from cooking, to buying, from wrapping to eating, has increased our awareness of what this celebration is all about, and has kept the weight off too; less trim on the tree and more trim on our waistlines. What else has this change in our traditional Christmas meant for us?

I can hardly explain the experience in words, as there is so much emotion flowing through my mind, heart and spirit. A genuine desire to help someone, a happiness overflowing out into our lives, a peaceful view of tomorrow, and a message of hope, love, and gratitude that we long to share with everyone we meet, these are just a few of the blessings received so far this Christmas. We have even more importantly gained a spiritual awakening together, my husband and I, like no other time of our lives. I am amazed at the closeness we feel to our Father in Heaven, his Son in the manger, and the Savior Jesus Christ as man, King, and Lord in and of our lives.

We will still have presents to share with others in our family and with our friends, I'm still cooking and enjoying the colorful decorations, yet they have completely taken a back seat to the reality of why we are celebrating Christmas and I have never been more blessed, felt more uplifted and joyful, or been as close to God. The moments of this year's Christmas will not be tied with ribbons, but tied in unity with my husband as we share an Advent devotion. My fondest memories will be those I spent in deep prayer not knee deep in wrapping paper. My greatest gift this year wasn't wrapped in bright paper but in swaddling clothes. There will be no need for gift exchanges and returns as Jesus Christ exchanged his gift of eternal life for me by taking my place on the cross.

Less is more I hear, and my husband and I are proving that this is really true as we are possibly celebrating the most wonderful Christmas season ever by having less, doing more, and opening up our hearts to receive the grace and mercy, love and peace that does not come delivered in the mail, in a tin of cookies or under a sparkling tree. We are excited to wake each morning with a new expectancy of a Savior born every day in our hearts, with a spiritual and emotional celebration of Jesus like in no other season, holiday, or time in our lives. I am grateful to be able to share this with you today through this devotion and invite you and yours to see if maybe a little less Christmas and a lot more Christ is right for you too...

# SIXTY-NINE

## Christmas Blues

Do you know anyone who gets a real case of Christmas blues? When everyone else seems to be merrily going their way humming carols and decking their halls, and they can hardly get out of bed for dread of all that is expected of them and from them. What about that feeling of being left behind or out of the holiday gatherings or shopping sprees? When people have made plans and totally forgotten that there are many who do not have anyone at all to share the holiday. It's Christmas and we should remember that there are those who are in need of a visit or even just a nod of hello, acknowledgement that they are important or at least not invisible. Whatever happened to peace on earth, good will to men? Wait a minute, that line came from scripture, not a Christmas anthem but an angel song.

What are some other holiday situations that can bring on those Christmas blues? Family that can't be with us or that doesn't want to be together, time off promised but not given, shortage of funds, just simply no spirit...wait...no spirit? I believe that is the number one reason for the Christmas blues. I wrote just the other day about having the Christmas spirit in you through the Holy Spirit, not you getting into the spirit, and the Christmas blues is typically what can happen when you begin to forget the reason for the season and leave Christ out of Christmas...how sad is this beloved, that we can allow the things of the world to overshadow the Holy Spirit and bring us to a point of depression....

What about the poor, the homeless, the hungry, sick and lonely? Don't they deserve a Christmas filled with cheer, happiness, joy and peace? Oh my yes, of course they do, but how about the rest of the year? What do they deserve then? What about those who cannot shake off the Christmas blues long after the holidays have passed? What are we doing for them? I believe it is time to rethink our idea of missions in a community where the lost and the believer alike need ministering to during the Christmas season and all year through. Visiting the nursing homes and hospitals, preparing and taking meals to homeless shelters, reaching out to the lonely and elderly of our churches, and generally following the words of Jesus Christ. Read Matthew 25:35-40...and of course to spread the gospel of Jesus Christ, every day, every opportunity.

It can be the most wonderful time of year or it can possibly be the most depressing. We are, or at least should be, responsible for having an awareness of what our brothers and sisters are dealing with, through compassionately caring about and watching out for their needs and concerns, at what can be the most difficult of times, Christmas. Reaching out to the lonely and down trodden, the sick and hurting can perhaps bring us closer to the true meaning of Christmas while putting us in a position to give back some of that, which we have been so richly blessed.

# SEVENTY

## Being Completed

God is completing me as I grow older...I have been "struggling" since I was a teenager to find a place in God's world, to know and understand his plans for my life. This week I will be turning fifty-seven and I may have finally realized that this whole time, my entire life, I have been working towards this moment. I am never going to be absolutely finished with the learning process, no one ever is; we continue to learn from the Father through the Holy Spirit until the last breath is drawn. What I do know that I did not know when I was much younger, is that in order for me to find a place of complete obedience, where my ministry on this earth can reach a maturity, I have to be open to the changes that God calls me to make.

These changes come in many different ways; through listening to my church family, my mentors, my spirit listening to God's voice, and through my own conviction that Christ's expectations from my life are never going to be different, his plans are unchanging, I am not. If I never change, if stay the same forever, then I will grow stagnant and wasteful...wasted time is a thing from my past not my future. With maturity comes expectations, from within myself and from God. I believe this past year has held a more sincere display of my own fulfillment than any other year of my life, and I am grateful for all the changes that I have had to make in order to see this happen.

Worry; a component of life, one that is never easily given up to God even though one continually tries to let go of it. All through my life I have held onto my fears, worrying about money, health, relationships and all the mysteries of this journey I am on. Now, as I accept my maturity, I can truly read the words from Luke 12:22-31 knowing that my worries are for naught, a waste of valuable time that could be best spent in my ministry, in God's work and in his Word.

I am grateful for this season in my life, my ongoing completeness of maturity fulfilling God's plan for my ministry, my journey, and most of all my personal realization, that it is all about Jesus, just Jesus. And I am excited to know that if his plans allow for it, I have much more to learn, to do, and to be in my changeable, maturing completeness...

# SEVENTY-ONE

# Christ Centered

"After all, this is what Christmas is all about!" This is a quote from a local television news anchor speaking about a "paying it forward" piece that had been reported on the show. I immediately thought about this and sadly realized, this is really what some people think, the time to give, to help others, comes once a year, Christmas. Now, I am not saying we shouldn't give at Christmas, we should, but paying it forward, helping those in need, is a responsibility we need to take seriously every day of the year. Hebrews 13:16 "And do not forget to do good and to share with others, for with such sacrifices God is pleased."

Christmas is all about one thing, the birth of Jesus Christ. "For God so loved the world that he sent his only son that whoever believes in him shall not perish but have eternal life"; that is the reason we celebrate, Christ's birth, that is the reason we set aside a special time of ceremony and services. The Christmas season has given mankind an opportunity to do all manner of good, a true season for giving and "paying it forward", but it should never become the reason for the season.

The birth of Jesus Christ, the holy aura of Immanuel, God with us, the love coming down for all mankind is easily lost as the traditional reason for this season, while we cover ourselves with the doing of good deeds, toys for tots, feeding the homeless, and "paying it forward". All worthy of our attention and giving every day of the year, and not a subtle way of obscuring the birth of Jesus Christ and his Holy and most significant birth.

Thank you God for not so subtly reminding me that I can get caught up in the hustle and bustle of the season, even with my own personal giving, forgetting to create a heart of humility and pure love, to celebrate the birth of our Savior, putting that at the top of my giving list, sharing his gospel. "Paying it forward" every day, giving from what I have so richly been blessed with, and keeping Christ as the center of my Christmas celebration and giving.

# SEVENTY-TWO

## I Love You

Oh my, here I go again. Another much to fast trip with those grandsons of mine, and my other family too, just kidding, I love them all. It may seem like, at times, that I favor the children, but they do require more attention than adults do and of course, have a most special place in my heart. But I love them all equally even though it was my nine year old grandson who woke up in the middle of the night saying, "I love you Nana."

This so reminds me of how our Father in Heaven loves us; you, me, our neighbors, the rude clerk in the store, the nasty mouth taxi driver in New York....Yes God loves us all the same. You and I, we may express our love for God more verbally than others, we may be a truer reflection of his love than others, we may be on a surer path than others, but that changes nothing from the fact that God loves them just as much as he loves us.

We are in the season of spreading love and good will, peace and harmony, the celebration of the birth of Jesus Christ. Have you noticed how much more often we hear, we say, I love you to those we may not bother to tell another time? I have, guilty as charged...I have found myself noticeably more cheerful, throwing out smiles and good wishes like I was a millionaire with plenty to spare. Oh, but wait, I am a millionaire, a billionaire even, when it comes to love and the great amount I have received from God. The fact is, the only way to keep receiving this great store of love is to give it away.

The greatest story of love is the one that begins with Christmas and ends with Easter, a story of love like no other. The living, dying, living, love of Jesus Christ and a love we would wise to emulate every day of the year, not just at Christmas alone. When I left my daughter's home this morning I didn't stop loving my grandsons, I love them more. I suspect, actually, I know that Jesus felt the same way when he left us to return to his Father. Every day, hour and minute that passes his love only grows stronger and more passionate for each of us, believer or not, he loves us all the same.

So here's to you beloved, I love you, yes you. To show my love in a more viable way than mere words let me say if there is anything you need prayer for please leave a comment on this post for me to lift you up to our Father and if you have never received one of my books, private message me your address and I will send you a copy of one in time for Christmas. I love you...

# SEVENTY-THREE

## The Holy Land Experience

The Holy Land Experience was wonderful and the displays, from wax figures to ancient artifacts were remarkably well done. From the first "shalom" to the last prayer spoken, it really was a time to reflect on the life of Christ and so much more, his death, sacrifice, and resurrection. I found a real connection with all the scripted scenes we watched throughout the day, particularly the very first the "Four women who loved Christ". The expression of emotions from each actress pulled me in reminding me of my own love and relationship with Christ and how deeply it has grown, how much I love him.

It was during the last performance, "The Passion of Christ" that I was moved the most, a not so subtle reminder of my son and Christ's forgiving and redeeming grace. The Roman soldier portrayed in the scene who was most vicious towards Jesus during the crucifixion broke down in overwhelming guilt and shame as they carried the body of Jesus away. He had a speech that was extremely in your face about how we ourselves treat our Savior and yet he forgives us all, and of everything, if we but ask.

In the final scene, "The Lamb's Book of Life", this same soldier was welcomed by Jesus Christ himself and a crown placed on his head, the reality of redeeming grace displayed in all its awesome splendor. Oh yes beloved, no matter what you may have done, who you are, were, or will be, God's forgiveness is that big; he forgave those who killed him, he forgives those today who would try to kill his name and his gospel, how much more forgiveness does he have for you and me? I sat in silence watching this play out in a scene for entertainment and evangelism, but inside my heart, mind and spirit were anything but quiet. I was crying out, yes God, yes; I have been guilty, will be guilty again, but washed clean by the redeeming blood of Jesus Christ, just as those who have all gone before me and have accepted his forgiveness and plan.

The Holy Land Experience was a good day, filled with lovely sights, sounds and smells, but more importantly it was a day filled with the Holy Spirit who spoke to everyone coming through the gates who would listen. "He who has an ear, let him hear what the Spirit says to the churches." Revelations 3:29 This is what I came away with from the day; listen to God as he has so much to say, open your heart to his truths and receive his amazing forgiveness.

# SEVENTY-FOUR

## Communion

What a privilege to prepare communion with my husband Sunday. As we gathered the components of the bread and the wine we carefully put together what our church family would be using to celebrate and consecrate the Lord's supper. Humbled by the emotional impact it was making on my heart I stopped for a moment to consider exactly what this privilege afforded me. I prayed that the Holy Spirit would reveal to me the truth behind the action of not only serving the church in this way but to convict me of anything that might be in the way of my own accepting the wine and the bread. I believe that you must come to the Lord's table with a sincere desire for the purpose of celebrating the sacrifice that Jesus Christ made for each of us and with a heart free of sin.

As we placed the wine (juice) and the bread (crackers) on the serving platters I was deeply touched by the poignant meaning of the moment. To be a small part of the ceremony was touching me in ways that participating in communion had never done before. Performing an act of service that has such significant impact on the congregation, their hearts joined together as one in the partaking of the Lord's supper was serving to remind me why I am service and have a ministry for our Lord. We read in Matthew chapter 26:26&28 "Take and eat; this is my body. This is my blood of the covenant, which is poured out for many for the forgiveness of sins." Oh precious lamb of God as we enter the season of celebrating your birth, help us not forget your sacrifice, the love that came down on Christmas for this reason alone; Savior of man.

I pray that as the days ahead get jumbled together with carols and jingles, with joy and greed, with lush decorations and simple mangers, that we will not forget the covenant of our Lord Jesus Christ. As I wiped clean the communion plates and placed them back upon their shelves I considered for a moment the reason for the season, not Christmas but Easter. Matthew 26:29 "I tell you, I will not drink from the fruit of the vine from now on until that day when I drink it new with you in my Father's kingdom." Help us Father God to remember that we cannot have the joy and excitement of Christmas and Mary bearing our Savior the baby Jesus, without remembering the pain and suffering that was bore by him, the grown man, Jesus Christ, on Easter.

# SEVENTY-FIVE

## Southern Living

I received my December issue of Southern Living magazine in the mail and excitedly skimmed through the holiday decorations, the gift section, hurriedly making my way to the "I'll be home for Christmas" cooking section. Throughout the house could be heard the sounds of "oohs and ahhhs" as my gaze fell onto page after page of delightful desserts, cookies, and dinner ideas placed upon the most amazing and elaborate table settings for any home at Christmas time. Thinking out loud I said, "This is the year! I am going to revamp my menu, out with the old recipes, the worn, boring, and ho hum dishes." Thumbing through the pages of delectable mouthwatering pictures I could just see myself in my new red dress, pearls and heels, placing the platter of cider braised pork shoulder along side of the butternut squash mash with the peppermint ribbon Christmas cake holding place of honor on the kitchen counter, while my family claps with pride and enthusiasm for my efforts. The reality of life is that the picture of this perfect Christmas scenario is no more going to happen then when I was a little girl circling with a crayon all the toys I wanted Santa to bring but I knew I would not get.

Christmas traditions. The idea of traditional are the flood of memories that come through doing basically the same time honored things, year in and year out, almost without exception. The same foods, goodies, decorations, the same lists checked once, twice, three times before the big day finally arrives. I love my old family favorites while my husband wants us to start our own traditions. So every year we try something different, whether it be a food or place, a decoration or gathering, I want to honor his idea for a traditional Christmas with something new. While neither of us have pictures of sugar plums dancing in our heads, neither do we have ideas of an extraordinary holiday with all the glitz and glitter of Southern Living magazine.

Whether I dress up in a new red outfit with high heels and pearls, create a sumptuous menu, or decorate my home in all the lush greenery and ribbons, my love for the season will remain fast with every memory from Christmas past. Every tradition only serves to emphasize the depth of happiness associated with Christmas, beginning when I was a child hoping for that one of a kind doll, to when my own children discovered the hidden stash of Santa in my closet, to today's holiday, watching my grandsons expectant faces light up underneath the tree lights. These are not the traditions of Christmas only the leftover residue from each one celebrated all so long ago.

Tradition is important for a healthy and successful holiday within the boundaries of personal design and desire trying to keep those ideals that we were taught and have continued to pass on to our families. My daydreaming about wearing a red dress and pearls is humorous only; I will most likely wear jeans and a sweater. What we do desire in the way of Christmas traditions is the spirit that comes with knowing who, what, and why, we celebrate with our favorite things, food, family, and music, the reason for the season; Jesus was born on Christmas morning.  Now we are getting to the real heart of the traditional season with all its celebration and customs, keeping Christ in Christmas.

A star upon the tree or maybe an angel, both are representatives of that wonderful wonderful night so long ago, serving to keep in our hearts and minds that a king was born. A crèche in the yard or a manger scene on the living room table remind us of the real people in the story; these are traditional displays of the true meaning and spirit of Christmas. The children practicing for the church play, learning their lines, all be it reluctantly, singing Christmas carols knowing only the first verse and chorus, these things are making memories and creating traditions. Visiting the shut ins from church or hospital bound patient, sharing the spirit of the season, here are true blessed traditions that make the holidays merry, bright, and bring them to life in our hearts and memories.

Where is Christ in Christmas when you fight the Black Friday crowds to save a dollar or two? Where is he when you end up in an argument with your spouse over where to hang the lights or whether to even put up a tree? Where is Christ when all around you all you can see is tinsel and ribbons, snowmen and Santas, dollar signs and drained bank accounts?  Where is the real spirit of the season?  It will not be found in a red dress or pearls, in exotic recipes and a dip in the bank account, nor underneath a brightly lit tree with an angel on top with the gaily wrapped presents waiting to be opened. Christ in Christmas is displayed in each of us as his light shines from within and out onto the world that tries so hard to remove him. Christ in Christmas is kept there, not by a mythical charm that appears once a year, but in the smiles given to the clerk who is struggling to get through a tough shift, the hands reaching out to help the needy, and by true believers sharing the gospel of Jesus Christ. These are the true and meaningful traditions of Christmas.

Traditional Christmas, laughter and happiness, song and cheer, food and giving; all these are wonderful ways to enjoy the holidays. Red dresses and pearls, fancy decorations and delectable meals all have a real place in some Christmas celebrations, maybe just not in my own. What does belong in all of the "twelve days of Christmas" is the Spirit of Christ. The baby in the manger born to be King of every  man's heart, the virgin birth and the angel visits, the shepherds in the fields and even the animals in the barn, all of these are the real traditions of Christmas that should be first and foremost what we think of when we begin to prepare our hearts for this coming and every Christmas.

# SEVENTY-SIX

## Struggling with loneliness in a media driven world

Do you struggle with loneliness or minor depression when everywhere you look it seems that everyone you know is busy, happy, and carefree? All your friends are moving and shaking up their neighborhoods. Your acquaintances and co-workers lead busy, active lives. It is all right there on your Facebook feed or someone is Tweeting about their exciting adventures every day as you sit lonely and alone in your house, at your desk or wherever you spend the biggest part of your day. First let me say, it is an illusion....and secondly, you are not alone.

To address the first, the illusion of media; it is clear that we are all caught up in this deception that because we are posting our busy and active lives on Facebook and Tweeting out our thoughts and expressions that it makes it true. For some it probably is the reality, but I believe that most everyone of us who spend a lot of time posting our lives on media are caught up in an illusion of our own making. Let's face it, when we log off we are heading back to the same ordinary day that we almost always have. Scrolling through Facebook to see what others are doing should cause you to feel togetherness, not more lonely than what you already experiencing.

I am a Facebook fan, not so much the Tweeting, and I have often found myself living vicariously through the posts of others. I can see how easy it is to become envious of those who seem to have it altogether, leading busy and important lives. I, myself, have a tendency towards depression and so understand completely how the lonely would and do, become sad and feeling like the world is passing them by while they stay stagnant and alone.

What I observe and have learned is that we are never alone as God is always with us, yes even you who have not yet understood or accepted Him into your life. Because you do not believe does not mean that He is missing in action, it simply means that you have not yet noticed that He is right there beside you. God created you and wants to be recognized as your Father, your companion, as well as Redeemer. When you realize this and come to accept Him, you will never again feel lonely. Isaiah 65:24 "Before they call I will answer; while they are yet speaking I will hear."

Loneliness and depression are real issues and in a media driven world we may find ourselves facing the fear that we are not busy enough, not good enough, as we see the lives of others flash by online and through all the new age media outlets. To know that God is with us, that we are never truly alone, can be what separates us from our insecurities and doubts and reveals the grace that His love for us would have us feel.

John 1:16 "And from his fullness we have all received, grace upon grace."

Deuteronomy 31:6 "Be strong and courageous. Do not fear or be in dread of them, for it is the LORD your God who goes with you. He will not leave you or forsake you."

# SEVENTY-SEVEN

## Lists

Lists...we all make them, and now, during the Christmas season more than any other time of the year I have them spread out everywhere.

I make a list for shopping for the holiday meals, baking for gift giving, goodies to devour here at home, lists for the gifts I will purchase and lists for all the extra to-do's I will have. I list my needs, my desires, my meetings, my dates, my...lists are an important part of my life. God too has listed His desires for my life clearly in His Word.

He listed His commandments openly in the Old Testament, and Jesus reminds us of them again in the New Testament. God impresses upon us lists of how we should treat each other and expect to be treated in the Proverbs. Jesus gives us lists of expectations for everyday living and the blessings to look forward to in the beatitudes, and we are given a complete list of all we need to protect ourselves from evil and disasters from the world in the full armor of God found in chapter six of Ephesians.

Lists are an intricate part of how we go about living our daily lives, but too, they are a vital part of our spiritual lives. Necessary to survive in this world, we are richly blessed in the Living Word by all the lists that the Lord has provided to guide us and keep us on our journey.

# SEVENTY-EIGHT

## Teacher or Student

Teach me Lord...I have prayed many times for God to fill me with knowledge and I can say with complete faith that He has answered me every time I asked. I see clearly how He has given me direction through my sisters in Christ and now more so then ever.

I have a dear friend who just recently taught me how to love a new fruit, kiwi, she introduced me to it at lunch one day, now she says, "on to star fruit." This was of course in fun but it was important to both of us as we realized we had faith in each other, her as teacher me as student. This we can now carry over into much more spiritually important avenues together. She is teaching me about compassion and love as her face simply glows with both. She teaches me self-control as I talk non-stop and she patiently listens, smiles and listens.

As I consider now all the other people who have been in and out of my life, allowing God to work through them, I am overwhelmed with emotion. I may not have recognized them as teachers but now that I have matured in my walk I can see how much I really did learn from each one of them. I will be more careful now to look for God's lessons through the wise eyes of an elder church member, I will think harder on the words from my sisters in Christ and I will observe closer the joy of the choir as they lift their voices in songs of praise. I will also be aware of my own actions and words for those who might be listening to me. Are you a teacher or a student?

Most likely, as am I, you are both; you have someone you look up to and someone that is looking up to you. Let us open our hearts and minds to learn all we can from each other, knowing that all good things come from God.

# SEVENTY-NINE

## Seeing My Savior

There are so many ways I see my Savior this morning.  I see Him as my Father and Creator, who gently and lovingly moves through my day, showing me all the wonders and beauty of His world.  I see Him as a brother who knowingly nudges me along during the trials of my life, guiding me safely and gracefully even during the hardest of times. I see Him as Man, encompassing all humanity, hanging on the tree of Calvary, bearing all the sins of my life upon His shoulders.  I see Him as my Redeemer, an empty tomb revealing the truth that He has risen and in doing this has given me everlasting life.  I see Him as King, standing at the right hand of God who is upon the throne of Heaven and Earth.  I am astounded by this thought; that I serve a God who allows me to see Him in so many revealing and powerfully moving ways.  Philippians 2:8-9 "And being found in fashion as a man, he humbled himself and became obedient unto death, even the death of the cross. Wherefore God also hath highly exalted him and give him a name which is above every name."

# EIGHTY

## Misplacing Things

I never have a pen or pencil handy when I need one. That is a crazy statement coming from a writer, yet it is true. As a writer I am constantly making notes, jotting down ideas, sentences and sometimes just one word, and so I grab the first pen I find and usually take it with me from room to room as I go about whatever I was doing before the "ideal thought" popped into my head. Inevitably, I leave the pen or pencil wherever I took it, and name it lost until I happen upon it once again.

I imagine it is the same thing for a lot of different people who have hobbies similar to mine, creating as they go through their day, needing the necessary tool at hand and always misplacing such items just as they are wanted. For instance, a chef, who needs those glasses as they are about to check out a new ingredient or recipe but cannot seem to find them. How about a gardener, laying their gloves or trowel down on one side of the yard just as they realize they are needed. I am sure that anyone who has a creative mind (which includes everyone) used for a hobby or as a profession, knows exactly what I mean.

Another thing I often do to myself is lose (misplace) things. This is an offshoot of the carrying things around while working at housework and having those creative juices flowing simultaneously. My glasses perched on the top of my head, left in the bedroom, even the bath, have caused me more aggravation then both my kids did as teens (Just kidding my kids were awesome teenagers).  I make notes for my writing, my to do list, and my groceries; I lose them. I change purses and inadvertently leave behind my favorite lipstick, only to be convinced I have lost it until I use that purse again. I lose socks in the washer, who doesn't, and can't find my the mate to my favorite pair of shoes until I clean out the closet. Oh, and did I mention, I lose more pens then Bic can produce in a day.

I realize that I am not alone with this dilemma of losing pens, notes, lipsticks and socks, and so I dedicate this short story to all of you who often find yourself in the same boat as I and have forgotten exactly how you got into it. Seriously, this is just a funny way of admitting I am normal. We all misplace things at some point in time, search high and low, tearing up the house just to find our glasses on the top of our heads or worse, on the end of our noses. So I would end this with one thought, but unfortunately I have forgotten exactly what that was....

# EIGHTY-ONE

## Christian Sisters, Christian Friends

I am blessed to have several good friends in my life, women of God who bless me in the knowing of them alone. They mentor me, love me, cry with me and laugh with me. Some of them are older, a couple of them are younger but I learn from them all equally as they share their lives with me. I consider them sisters as well as friends, just as I consider my earthly sister a dear friend and a sister in spirit. It is a lovely feeling to reach out to one of these wonderful women and know that they pray when asked, listen when I need to talk and talk when they know I need to listen.

I am grateful to each one of them and would like to pay honor to them in this blog. One is a mentor who has seen much physical pain yet she is a shining example of how God works in our lives as He heals and blesses us. One is a go to lunch friend that although we may not see each other very often we pick up our conversations right where we left the last time we visited. Another is watching me, I just know she is, I pray for guidance every time we are together. Still another is a long distance friend. She and I rarely see each other or talk but let a birthday roll around and hers is the first card I will receive. I wish I could talk about them all and more broadly then in this posting, but I will end with one friend that God has recently brought into my life. She and I share a special bond, we are both artists; myself with the stroke of pen on paper and her with stroke of paintbrush on canvas. We have many other things in common but one thing she shares with me and everyone else she comes into contact with is her heart. If this makes you think of that special friend or friends in your life then take a moment to say I love you and make plans to get together soon.

Colossians 3:12-14 "Put on then, as God's chosen ones, holy and beloved, compassionate hearts, kindness, humility, meekness, and patience, bearing with one another and, if one has a complaint against another, forgiving each other as the Lord has forgiven you, so you also must forgive. And above all these put on love, which binds everything together in perfect harmony." Sweet harmony; a friend is part of your heart and therefore your heart-song. Thank you Lord for all these wonderful women, Christian sisters, that you have allowed to come into my life.

# EIGHTY-TWO

## Despair

Where are you today God? I looked for you with eyes that could not see. I listened for you with ears that could not hear. I felt for you with hands that could not touch. I moved through my day ever aware that your presence was not where I was. How can this be? I prayed, beseeching the Lord to reveal Himself to me. I heard nothing in response.

My spirit was in despair and my heart was breaking. Desperate I reached for His Word and stumbled through the pages grasping at any of the verses that might make Him draw near to me. The Word opens to Psalm 19: "The heavens declare the glory of God; the skies proclaim the work of his hands. Day after day they pour forth speech; night after night they reveal knowledge. They have no speech, they use no words; no sound is heard from them. Yet their voice goes out into all the earth, their words to the ends of the world."

Suddenly all is revealed; I was seeking God with blind eyes, deaf ears and unfeeling fingers. I rushed outside and looked up to the heavens and my spirit soared with knowledge of my Lord. There, I could see him in the wind whispering through the trees, I could hear him in the song of the birds, and I could feel Him down to the very depths of my soul. My God lives in me and through me and in everything that exists if I only use the faith that was born in me. Have you ever experienced this feeling of despair? I believe God is calling you today to look, listen and feel His mighty works and to draw Him nearer to you with a spirit of desire and thankfulness.

# EIGHTY-THREE

## Relationships

Consider the people in your life; each and every one in whom you have had any relationship, no matter how long. There are those that we have but a fleeting time with and then some that have been with us our entire lives. Do you believe that God has a plan for you? People come in and out of lives for a reason. We may not always understand how God uses them, but we can be assured that He does. There are the clouds in your life. These people that float in and out like soft fluffy clouds or even those that rage through quickly like the storm clouds. What they have in common is that they make a huge impact and then suddenly are gone.

There are any number of reasons that you need this short but important relationship, a neighbor or co-worker, even a stranger can bring a blessing that has a long term affect on the rest of your life. It is not always the quantity of time spent with them but the quality. You may never measure their worth in your life, but God has. There are the flowers in your life. A beautiful surprise that bursts with color and aroma and lingers for just a while but makes a huge difference in your life. A lovely friend or a Sunday school teacher; their presence lifts you up and bring so much pleasure while they are with you. Though they may not have a permanent place in your life, oh what joy they bring while they are with you. These are the trees in your life. Firmly planted friends or family; they are a true fixture and you trust them throughout all times and all the changes that you go through as you live out the plan God has provided.

These people provide shade in your summertime and color to your falls, simply by the love that is a part of what makes them who they are to you. The trees in your life can be cut down and removed because even with the deepest of roots there is a season for all things. Death will take a parent, a career can move your best friend; but even when you no longer have them in your life you will always have them in your heart. There are the rocks in your life. Solid, trustworthy and deeply imbedded in our lives. A mentor or pastor, your parent or spouse, even best friend. No matter what the circumstance we know that if anyone shows any real accountability in our lives it is our rocks. Dependable, knowledgeable, spiritual and steadfast; our rocks are ever present, even in death, they are still with us. These are the anchors in your life. There is one mountain in your life. An immovable stronghold, with the highest of reaches who embodies all the characteristics of the clouds, flowers, trees and rocks. This is God. He floats through your day as the Holy Spirit moves you, he brings with Him the surprise of the beauty of His creation, He is permanent, and He is your rock and anchor.

EIGHTY-FOUR

Refugees

Refugees, by the very definition means a person who flees persecution, is displaced or in exile. The Syrian refugee status has been on the news, in the media and if you are like me, on our minds for a couple of weeks. Our pastor made a statement concerning this subject and as he spoke it occurred to me that what he was describing was exactly how my husband and I have been feeling since deciding to leave one church in search of a new one. We felt displaced and as if in some way we were in exile, one of our own making. Mind you we were following the leading of the Holy Spirit making this decision but nevertheless we felt lonely and like a refugee without a home.

When you make a decision to leave a church you are leaving behind family, you are saying goodbye to all that is comfortable and known, and you create an empty space in your heart as you are now not serving God in His house. Much like the refugees seeking asylum from oppression, we were beginning to create an oppression of our own. We visited different churches and in each one we felt welcome but unfortunately we also felt like outsiders. This was of no fault to any one church but simply because we were temporarily displaced.

Comparing our situation to those of today's refugees is beyond ludicrous, yet, I have actually come to realize a little better how they feel in the most general sense of the word refugee. We needed a home. A church where we knew, that not only did we feel accepted but we knew that the Lord was guiding us there by the Holy Spirit speaking to us. He has, we believe, and that feeling of being displaced has vanished. We are grateful.

To close I leave you with this thought and two scriptures. We all absolutely, without a doubt will experience the feeling of being a refugee, being displaced and maybe even persecuted. We have a power in us that separates us from the typical refugee of today's world, we have the Holy Spirit. He is moving us, encouraging us and as long as we seek Him first we will not be refugees for very long.

Psalms 59:16 "But I will sing of your strength; I will sing aloud of your steadfast love in the morning. For you have been to me a fortress and a refuge in the day of my distress."

Psalms 119:10 "With my whole heart I seek you; let me not wander from your commandments!"

# EIGHTY-FIVE

# Thanksgiving

Psalm 100
Make a joyful noise to the LORD, all the earth! Serve the LORD with gladness! Come into his presence with singing! Know that the LORD, he is God! It is he who made us, and we are his; we are his people, and the sheep of his pasture. Enter his gates with thanksgiving, and his courts with praise! Give thanks to him; bless his name! For the LORD is good; his steadfast love endures forever, and his faithfulness to all generations. "Enter His court with praise and

On this Thanksgiving day, more than any other time in my life, I can say these words with authority and wisdom manifested through the Holy Spirit. I will not break each verse down, which is my usual devotion, but ask you, the reader, to go back and read these words again for yourself. I'll wait.

This psalm encompasses not merely what we, children of God, should be expressing today, on Thanksgiving, but every day of our lives. Joy, singing, gladness, these are our true emotions, our true nature. Service, praise, being in His will (sheep of His pasture); these make up our responsibility to Him who gives us everything, for all that He does, has done and will do for each of us. Thanksgiving, come before prepared, each day, to thank Him, in His court, which implies bended knees. God is good and His love unchanged throughout the generations of the earth.

Thanksgiving is a time of gathering together with family and friends to share a meal, visit with those who we love, and it is a day set aside to thank God. Thank Him for another year of blessings and joy, through the rough patches, the disasters near and far, and through everyday life. The promise that God gives those who serve Him is one that urges, compels, a grateful heart to have thanksgiving every day. Enter His gates with thanksgiving and His court with praise. That beloved, is thanksgiving each and every day.

I leave you with a thought as we fast approach the season of gladness and joy. Maybe each day should be a day of thanksgiving in your heart. Put aside the hustle and bustle that would crush your spirits, and say thank you Lord. Put aside the decorating and gift wrapping and say thank you Lord. Put aside the worry and anxiety of the holiday season and say thank you Lord. Thanksgiving throughout the Christmastide, thanksgiving for the reason that we celebrate, His Son, our Redeemer, Jesus Christ.

# EIGHTY-SIX

## Christmas Greens

Decorating for Christmas and making a salad are very similar even with their dissimilarities. They have three things in common; they both involve the use of greens, no two people put them together in the same way, and we believe that it is so good for us that we gorge on them. Who hasn't been to the salad bar at least twice to indulge? While decorating for Christmas don't we usually see something that isn't quite right so we put up more decorations to fill in the gaps. We over-indulge on decorating. Salad is healthy for our bodies and Christmas decorations serve to put the spirit into the holiday. Back up a minute. Is salad, when you hit the bar for the third time and heap on the cheese and dressing really good for you? Is the spirit of Christmas truly in the decorating?

We eat those greens, veggies and toppings, enjoying the taste, color and healthy choice we made. We hang the greens of Christmas, wreaths, garland and trees, absorbing the spirit of the holiday season. So similar too in the emotions that they bring to us. The typical garden salad; beautifully arranged on the plate gives one the satisfaction of eating healthy while looking so pretty with the colors of fresh vegetables. The Christmas tree; lit with gleaming colored or golden lights, where upon each branch hang favorite family ornaments handed down from generation to generation. Different emotions from each but satisfying in the way they make us feel about our lives and ourselves.

As I begin my decorating for Christmas I consider what joy is found in each piece that I display; my mantel gracefully holding my Nativity scenes, the kitchen alive with snowmen that the hottest oven will not melt and my tree adorned with ornaments from all my travels and gifts from family and friends. Memories mix with happy thoughts of the coming season to remind me that just as the eating of the salad doesn't make me healthy, the decorating for Christmas doesn't give me the true spirit. It is a start, and a good one. Salad can be healthy when paired with a good daily diet, decorating for Christmas can be a good way to usher in the holidays when paired with the reason for the season.

Just as we challenge our bodies to accept the healthy idea of the salad bar, the greens and ingredients for a well put together meal, we prepare our hearts for holiday cheer that we receive as we decorate. What we come to realize is the promise of the Christmas season begins not with the decorations, not in the food or in the gifts, but begins in the center of it all, the spirit of hope, peace, comfort and joy. These are things which belong to every heart when preparing for the season. So we celebrate the hanging of the greens, representing everlasting life, the life given by the Son of God and man, whose birthday is the reason for the season.

# EIGHTY-SEVEN

## Enjoyment

God created you for His enjoyment. Is He enjoying your life? Have you stopped to consider if the life you are leading is bringing pleasure to Him? Is what God sees you doing, being, what He wants from you? We ask Him, praying, "What is your will for me?" God responds revealing His plans through the gifts He created us with, through the leaders He has provided to us, and through His Word when we study with steadfast prayer commitment. Our omnipotent God, our Father, Creator, is watching, prompting us to always do and be what His intended purpose for us was when He formed us in our mother's womb.

Revelations 11:4 Thou art worthy, O Lord, to receive glory and honor and power: for thou has created all things and for thy pleasure they are and were created.

We have all, at one time or another, questioned our purpose, struggled to stay on that straight and narrow. Remembering that God is in control, that His eyes are always upon us, and His Holy Spirit with us should bring us fear in the form of awe and respect. To know that God our Father, created us for the good works that we do, the love we share, should be enough to keep our feet planted firmly on the ground of His will. Does your life bring glory and honor to God who alone is worthy? Is God enjoying your life?

Ephesians 3:10 "For we are his workmanship, created in Christ Jesus for good works, which God prepared beforehand, that we should walk in them."

God created you for His enjoyment. Is He enjoying your life? Interesting question. As I sit in quiet obedience, writing this, I admit that often I have questioned the point of continuing with my ministry; that is simply the truth. God's Word continually shows me something different. God created me for His pleasure, and He clearly shows me that, through His Word when I take time and prayerfully seek His will.

God created you for His enjoyment. Is He enjoying your life? The scriptures below have recently given me back my focus. If you find this message is for you today, then I leave them for you to increase your knowledge and encourage you to know that God created you for His pleasure.

Philippians 2:4-5
Psalm 40

# EIGHTY-EIGHT

## Christmas Past

We all have memories from Christmas past that serve to remind us of our joy, laughter, and the abundant grace that fills our hearts with love again and again. There are also memories of those Christmases that left you feeling underwhelmed and joyless. I have a memory of my father's tears one Christmas when I was a child and it is one that I have never forgotten.

Although it is sad, I cannot help pulling it out year after year and examining the events of a celebration that brought him so much pain through no fault of his own. A family gathering and everyone, adults and children alike received gifts; I remember clearly tearing into mine excited for what I would find. It was not until much later that I realized that my father did not receive a gift, he alone had been forgotten. I and a brother were exposed to his pain and grief when he laid it down at the feet of his mother. We sat on her living room sofa while around the corner in her kitchen he cried as if his heart was broken, and of course it was.

My brother and I disobeyed our Father's order to stay in the living room of course and silently and timidly stole our way to the kitchen door. My grandmother held my father in her arms while he cried and I do not remember what she was saying to him as I was caught completely off guard as a six year old watching her father cry. What I did see, most likely for the very first time in my life, was crushing hurt, and more importantly, the suggestion that even adults need someone to turn to when the pain they are suffering, whether emotional or physical, is more than they can bear.

We have a Father in Heaven who would hear our prayers, in a constant and consistent flow, and too, He would readily hold us in His arms when we have a painful experience and are overwhelmed by the emotional impact on our hearts and souls. A compassionate and loving God who sees our hearts, knows our suffering, and cares. Just as my grandmother was waiting for my father to pour out his grief, God is waiting to receive ours. Whether emotional or physical, even when we think He may have more vital prayers to attend, God cares for every tear that falls. Psalms 56:8 "You have kept count of my tossings; put my tears in your bottle. Are they not in your book?"

I will never forget my father's tears; it silently broke my heart, although I do not believe he ever knew. Nor does God forget our tears as we cry out in desperate need, or when we silently suffer and cry alone. I am so grateful for our Father who is waiting, always waiting, for us to come into His arms for comfort, compassion and love. Always love, a love that never fails. Psalms 36:7 "How precious is your steadfast love, O God! The children of mankind take refuge in the shadow of your wings."

# EIGHTY-NINE

## Perfection

Trying to be perfect in an imperfect world is something I believe that we all struggle with at one time or another. The idea of perfection, as identified in scripture, is found in Matthew 5:48 "You therefore must be perfect, as your heavenly Father is perfect. We also read in James 1:4 "And let steadfastness have its full effect, that you may be perfect and complete, lacking in nothing." The word perfect here has the meaning of mature. In other words, be mature in an immature world. That sounds like something easier to accomplish, but is it?

Non-believers will quickly point out our flaws just as they will call us out if they think we are judging. Caught in the middle of light and dark in today's world can prove hard, but not impossible. Looking at perfection as maturity is a more objective way to enable us to share the truth without seeming to be "holier than thou". Once again look at the Word, 1 Peter 1:15 "but as he who called you is holy, you also be holy in all your conduct." So maybe the "holier than thou" remark has a place in the truth. But what a fine line we cross as we, mature, perfected, holy, Christians, walk through a world where we struggle to shine the line of Christ. And is that not the ultimate goal of every believer, to shine the light of Jesus?

Leviticus 19:2 ""Speak to all the congregation of the people of Israel and say to them, You shall be holy, for I the LORD your God am holy." God told Moses to tell the Israelites, not to be holy, but that they shall be holy. That was a command. To be a part of the family of God they would have to be holy, mature, perfected. We, adopted into this, God's family, are under the same command, be holy. God expects, demands, that we are mature, holy, creatures, ready to accept the responsibilities of being one of His holy people. Those responsibilities begin with maturing into our discipleship.

Colossians 1:28 "Him we proclaim, warning everyone and teaching everyone with all wisdom, that we may present everyone mature in Christ." Everyone! You beloved and me, we are to be presented as mature in Christ. Holy? Yes. Perfect? Yes that too. Trying to be perfect in an imperfect world? As a child of the one true God, we are being perfected as we mature into our holy selves. Shine that light sister, be bold brother. Walk through this dark world the perfect reflection of Jesus Christ, mature in His Word and holy in His Spirit.

# NINETY

## Fragrances

I was baking for Christmas yesterday and the house was filled with the aromas that can only be associated with the traditional holiday treats. Cinnamon, nutmeg, and peanut butter, yes I said peanut butter; these make up for my house the smells of Christmas. They bring much pleasure to us, reminders of Christmas past and excitement for Christmas present. As we take in the pungent fragrances of our kitchens we are filled with the knowledge that this year will be celebrated as we are accustomed, as our memories serve to reveal.

There are many scriptures throughout God's Word that speak of aroma or fragrances but there was one in particular that I was led to use. 2 Corinthians 2:14 "But thanks be to God, who in Christ Jesus always leads us in triumphal procession, and through us spreads the fragrance of the knowledge of him everywhere." God asked me, "What aroma is your ministry giving off this Christmas?" Have I sought to teach sound doctrine that has its focus set upon leading others to the knowledge of Jesus? Is my writing revealing that testimony which is helpful in producing fruit for God? My prayer is that the fragrance of my ministry of writing is always spreading an aroma of truth, hope and love. I pray the fragrance is one of grace.

I challenge you now, beloved readers, to think on this present Christmastime and consider what fragrance that you may be spreading as you go about your daily routine. With a bit of holiday Spirit we can share the gospel of Jesus Christ in an aromatic and fragrant way that those who have yet to believe will see Him in us. As we share our homemade fudge, cookies and cakes, we can add a fragrance that lingers long after the cinnamon and nutmeg have faded. The fragrances of knowing Jesus Christ as Lord and Savior. Sharing His love is the very best of gifts anytime of the year, so allow His lovely aroma to surround every present you wrap and let His fragrance be the smells of Christmas.

# NINETY-ONE

## Messes

I walked in the backdoor struggling with several tote bags filled with groceries for all the Christmas baking I had planned and what to my tired eyes did appear, a countertop smeared with peanut butter and bread crumbs, an empty milk glass and the kitchen sink left with the mornings breakfast dishes. My first thought was an angry one; oh that husband of mine! Beginning to feel like a martyr, I started that mumbling under my breath, you know what I mean. Before I could get the first syllable out the Holy Spirit convicted me, right there on the spot.

God sees the messes I leave behind on a daily basis and yet I feel only acceptance and love coming from Him. Compared to the mess my husband sometimes leaves, I should feel beyond grateful that God allows me to leave those that I often do. I have tried to help my husband by leaving hints, being upfront and just saying, please clean up your messes, but sometimes he forgets, and I know that I need to forgive him and I do.

God, even as He created us, saw all the mistakes that we would make as we move through this life leaving one mess after another. The amazing thing is that He loves us through them all. He loves us enough to have prepared a way for us to not only learn to tidy up after ourselves but to not leave the messes at all. What way is that, you ask? It is the truth and the light, Jesus Christ. The very reason that I need a savior is the same reason why God sent His only Son. Yes, Jesus helps us clean up all the messes of our lives and assists in keeping us from repeating them.

So now I think about my mess making husband, who really doesn't mean to leave bread crumbs and empty glasses behind for me to find, and I smile. Next time I happen upon a mess he leaves I will remember how much God loves me, enough that not only does He forgive me, but He has prepared a way for me not to ever leave another mess behind. Now, if I can just think of way to get my husband to remember to wipe off the kitchen countertop...

# NINETY-TWO

## The Color Blue

I had a blue Christmas this year; not one with an emotional connection but in the way that most of the presents I received were the color blue. All shades of blue: turquoise, my favorite of all colors, eggshell blue, royal blue, and baby boy blue. The sparkling gifts all open and placed strategically to show off their brilliance serve to remind me of the love I receive from family and friends, and the abundant grace that God has poured into my life throughout this past year. I am grateful that my blue Christmas is representative of only love and not loneliness from missing someone or something.

As I think on all these unique shades of blue I consider what the color blue means to me and how it might be represented in God's Word. After a little research I did find several references to blue in the Old Testament, most especially when it came to the priests and their robes. Looking in Numbers I discovered that God had commanded the Israelites to place blue tassels on the sleeves of the priests robes. This was to serve as a reminder to keep His commandments. Numbers 15:39 "And it shall be a tassel for you to look at and remember all the commandments of the LORD, to do them, not to follow after your own heart and your own eyes, which you are inclined to whore after."

Strong words of admonishment to a people who God had recently led through the desert out of Egypt, freeing them from hundreds of years of bondage. These words serve as a reminder to myself in the coming year to follow God's will in my life, seeking forgiveness when necessary, to always show love and share the gospel at every opportunity that presents itself. God's commandments echo throughout time and the knowledge and acknowledgement of Jesus Christ as my Savior, has washed me not the color of blue but white, as white as snow.

I know that as I continue down this pathway I will definitely encounter some blue skies along the way. Blue, the color of royalty, blue the way pointing to heaven, blue the color of my life. Yes I had a blue Christmas and acknowledge the extreme blessings I received from those who thought about me and honored me with their choices of the color blue in my gifts. I am even more honored that God, as He always does, nudged my spirit to consider what this meant to my heart, these gifts in shades of blue.

# NINETY-THREE

## Putting Away Christmas

Putting away Christmas...packing up the lights, taking down the greenery, the wreaths and lastly the tree. It seems sad in a way to have it end so soon, at least it seems too soon to this one woman. Yet I know that Christmas is not ever completely put away as it lingers on in the hearts of all believers. We find it in the sky as the glimmer of the star of Bethlehem steadily shines. The promise of the Christ Child grown has our hearts racing towards Easter and the most precious gift of all. The sacrifice begun with love coming down from a heavenly home realizes its fullness in the sacrifice of Calvary.

The joy that we receive during this season of love and giving must be held onto as it may easily slip away. Unlike our fruit of the spirit, which is born from the sanctification of our spirits, the fruit of Christmas is that extra joy received when we participate with real Christmastime spirit. So, let's be wary of packing away the joy and love we have in abundance at Christmas as we pack away the trimming and ornamental traces of the season.

Search your heart today and discover the fruit of Christmas flowing through your spirit, your mind and your soul. Every gift you gave, brings joy. Every smile shared, brings joy. Every child's happy face, brings joy. The light of Jesus created through the advent of the season should continue to bring you joy that is unattainable in any other realm or way. Do not pack it away with the wrapping paper, the bows and the Christmas knick knacks. It must mean, it does mean, so much more of the joy of life than the fleeting memories of Christmas decorations and forgotten Christmas gifts.

John 15:11 "These things I have spoken to you, that my joy may be in you, and that your joy may be full." Christ is our joy. The joy that is from everlasting to everlasting. The Christmas season is but a fleeting moment in the year, one that creates overwhelming joy that continues to pour into us with the true meaning of Christmas.

# NINETY-FOUR

# The Cross

The cross has become one of the most recognizable symbols of Christianity. More importantly than the symbol that it is, how often is it during a day that we use the cross? We must always recognize the vital role it will play when used as our place to kneel, for the example of sacrifice that it reflects, and for the shared remembrance it stands for in each brother and sister in Christ. These are only some of the amazing thoughts we should have when considering the cross. More than thoughts and symbols, the cross is our way of life.

1 Corinthians 1:18 "For the word of the cross is folly to those who are perishing, but to us who are being saved it is the power of God." Therein lays the purpose of kneeling at the cross, for it has power unattainable in any other realm. The word of the cross is the gospel of Jesus Christ and is where every testimony should begin and end. The cross is so much more than a wearable symbol to those who know Jesus and have accepted the sacrifice He made hanging upon that tree. It is a place; a place where we come to know God, where we worship Him and we testify for Him.

Galatians 2:20 "I have been crucified with Christ. It is no longer I who live, but Christ who lives in me. And the life I now live in the flesh I live by faith in the Son of God, who loved me and gave himself for me." This is no symbolic life change, but a real thundering, ground shaking event and wearing a piece of golden jewelry around one's neck is merely scratching the surface as to the true meaning of the cross. We have to hang upon that tree! We have to die to self! We have to testify before man that it is no longer ourselves but Christ who lives in us. That beloved is what the cross means.

Much like the service of Communion, the cross reminds us of the sacrifice made by Jesus Christ for each one of us, believer and non-believer. Think upon the blood and body, reflect on the cross. Listen to the words of Jesus and allow the depth of meaning to flow through you. Matthew 10:38 "And whoever does not take his cross and follow me is not worthy of me." We must be willing to sacrifice as He sacrificed, giving everything we are; not as a symbol but for the testimony of what being a Christian, a follower of Jesus truly means.

# NINETY-FIVE

## Treasures

Proverbs 2:3-5 "yes, if you call out for insight and raise your voice for understanding, if you seek it like silver and search for it as for hidden treasures, then you will understand the fear of the LORD and find the knowledge of God."

How badly do you want spiritual knowledge, insight and understanding? Are we willing to seek it as we do the things of the world? We work hard at our careers, we struggle to raise families, we have needs and desires that without effort we can neither achieve nor retain. We want to see growth in every area of our lives: all things better than last year, happier than ever, financial freedom, love and health. These are all good commendable wishes and completely normal as we all aspire to better lives. So back to the original question; how much do you want spiritual treasure?

Matthew 6:19a & 21 "Do not lay up for yourselves treasures on earth. For where your treasure is, there your heart will be also." Jesus' words admonish those who clearly place more value on things of the world rather than things of the heart and spirit. Emphasizing treasure, we understand that anything we regard to be worthy is counted treasure and to be considered gain. Wisdom in the Word, studying to show ourselves approved, growing closer to God and maturity of the spirit are all treasures that assist us as we add to those things we store away in heaven. Additionally, we understand that knowledge is treasure that we can depend on today, right now during this time in our lives.

Proverbs 4:13 "Keep hold of instruction; do not let go; guard her, for she is your life." Throughout our lives we continue to learn and gather wisdom, becoming mature adults. Our spiritual selves are no different; we must never stop seeking God's instruction as we have to know exactly what His will is for our ministries and our own future. What we learn we must retain in order for it to become part of our stored treasure. "For she", instruction, is our lives, and without the wisdom received from the Word we seek the things of the world rather than things of the spirit.

God I pray for a heart that recognizes that the only treasure I need is you. Continue to open my eyes and heart to your Word, give me listening ears to know your voice and to count every piece of wisdom imparted in me as treasure to be guarded as the true riches it is.

# NINETY-SIX

## Inspiration

What inspires you? What is it that gets you motivated to action?

My husband was motivated by his knee pain to pursue replacement surgery, which led to him being inspired to research what it would involve, and then he motivated himself to pre-plan by doing rehab, going to the gym to regain lost upper body strength. I cannot say how impressed I am by his motivation and inspiring attitude towards the upcoming surgery. So as I consider how his pain created an inspired decision which led to motivated actions, I realize that this is exactly what we need to do in order to keep ourselves in a creative and interactive attitude towards our spiritual life.

Motivation; the reason or reasons that one has for acting or behaving in a certain way. Inspiration; the process of being mentally stimulated to do or feel something, especially when it comes to being creative. So as to our spiritual life, what is the reason, the motivation, for behaving as a Christian? That is an easy one, Jesus, or our desire to please God is or should be our motivation, along with our love for our fellow man. Our Inspiration? The stimulation of the Holy Spirit is our inspiration and knowledge of all the saints who have gone before us.

So Jesus motivates us and the Holy Spirit inspires us, can it really be that simple or could there be more to it? We were motivated by something in the beginning, before we first believed, and that is our sin conscious and our desire for a Savior. Yes, many fight this desire, and unfortunately, many completely ignore the nudging of their spirits to recognize the need, but this truth, the need for forgiveness, much like my husband's need to be free of pain, is our motivation for salvation, for our new life and for the change that we are now inspired to make.

We have to stay inspired, and we need to continue to feel motivated for our ministries, so we once again turn to the Holy Spirit and to the Word of God for everything we could possibly need to ensure that we do. Our spirits crave closeness with the Creator, our Father. This alone is a motivator, yet unless we are listening and recognize the inspiration of the Holy Spirit we will miss out on the opportunity for boundless hope, joy and love that we should be attaining.

What inspires you? What is it that gets you motivated to action? Is it a longing for peace and comfort, freedom from sin, or is your spirit crying out for its Creator? Like my husband was motivated by the pain in his knee, inspired to do whatever it takes to be stronger, better, active again, we should always be motivated to do whatever God asks of us and be inspired by the Holy Spirit to be stronger, better, more active Christians.

# NINETY-SEVEN

# Our Daily Bread

Matthew 6:11 "Give us this day our daily bread." What was Jesus speaking of when He told the disciples to pray for daily bread? Was He saying ask for food, substance for the body or was He saying ask for the bread of life, which is of course found only in Him? I believe that with careful attention to every word that Jesus spoke we can not only understand Him and His words, but we can receive the true fuel that we need to get through each day.

John 6:35 "Jesus said to them, "I am the bread of life; whoever comes to me shall not hunger, and whoever believes in me shall never thirst." There then is our daily bread. Christ says that only whosoever believes in Him shall not hunger nor thirst as He is the bread of life. It is Jesus who sustains us; He gives us everything we need, nothing is left out, from the nourishment of our souls to the nourishment of our bodies. Give us our daily bread Jesus, nourish us.

Matthew 4:4 "But he answered, "It is written, "'Man shall not live by bread alone, but by every word that comes from the mouth of God.'" Here we come to terms with the idea of the importance of nourishment for our souls versus our bodies. We cannot be sustained in this life on the things of the earth; yes we need our bodies nourished, but without the daily bread found in Jesus Christ our souls will starve and the body will no longer even matter. For what is life if all we focus on feeding is our bodies and not our spirits?

Matthew 26:26 "Now as they were eating, Jesus took bread, and after blessing it broke it and gave it to the disciples, and said, "Take, eat; this is my body." Every meal we partake of there should be consciousness of the source. As communion represents the blood and body sacrifice of our Savior, so should every meal we eat to sustain our bodies remind us of the truth, that all we have, all that is provided to us to sustain life in every way is through Him, Jesus Christ.

Give us this day our daily bread, which is you Jesus. Feed us your Word to fill our spirits with everything we could possibly need to sustain life. We cannot live by bread for our bodies alone but need the nourishment for our souls that comes from only you. Finally, help us O Lord to always remember the sacrifice made by you for each of us and to always be grateful for the bread that sustains all life, from physical to spiritual. You are our sustaining bread, our daily bread.

# NINETY-EIGHT

## Exercise

Without constant use we lose the muscle in our bodies and thus the need for exercise is understood. We walk, run, and do all sorts of movement to keep our muscles limber and healthy. Our heart is the hardest working muscle in our bodies and it too needs exercise in order to keep it healthy, functioning at its very highest level. Faith, the seed that has been planted in each and every one of us, needs to be used as well. Hebrews 11:1 defines faith for us so that we may naturally and successfully exercise our faith day in and day out. "Now faith is the assurance of things hoped for, the conviction of things not seen."

In order for our spirits to grow in wisdom and hope we absolutely have to exercise our faith. We go through this life with the belief that we have in Jesus Christ, a belief that could not have been born at all without that measure of faith. Yet, there is so much more to know, to discover and to believe as we grow; grow in the faith. 2 Corinthians 5:7 "for we walk by faith, not by sight." We must exercise our faith, that muscle of the spirit, through which we may discern those marvelous things that we would not be able to discover without it. With a growing and evolving faith, which happens when we exercise it, we will be so less likely to stumble and will not fall.

John 20:29 "Jesus said to him, "Have you believed because you have seen me? Blessed are those who have not seen and yet have believed." The beginning of such faith exercising is in the very words of Christ Himself. To have faith to believe without seeing Jesus is what some may call truly the ultimate leap of faith. When we first believe, the seed of faith will first appear. It is then that we must use faith to feel it growing in us as we study to show ourselves approved, love as Jesus loves, and complete the walk upon the pathway that He will set our feet upon. Exercise your faith in order to become a mature Christian and to not become stagnant, showing no growth.

Romans 1:17 "For in it the righteousness of God is revealed from faith for faith, as it is written, "The righteous shall live by faith." Exercise your faith.

Hebrews 10:38 "but my righteous one shall live by faith, and if he shrinks back, my soul has no pleasure in him." Exercise your faith.

Let us take time each day to exercise our faith through, prayer, study, worship and service. We should live by faith, partaking of Jesus as our daily bread, and fully integrate the fruit of the spirit as part of our daily regimen for living healthy Christian lives.

# NINETY-NINE

## Love Letters

I cannot imagine anything more appealing than love letters. Sweet, old fashioned, hand written, love letters, tied up in red ribbon with postmarks from another city, state, or country, those long forgotten letters filled with emotion and love. The smell of the paper and ink as you open, the crisp feel of the sheets beneath your fingers and the whisper of sweet something's wafting up from the words written in a spidery hand. These qualities of hand written letters, love letters or not, cannot be replicated by emailing and texting today, they simply do not hold the same sentiments even though I use these methods of communication myself.

The idea of a love letter is one that is a way to not only communicate one's feelings to another it was a way to mark the passing of time while sharing your life together. The words of a love letter tell the story of relationship between the writer and the receiver. Capturing on paper impressions of present hope, dreams of what may one day be, and collecting details of what has passed; a stack of messages written from one hand to another's heart. I have a love letter written to my mother from my grandmother, her mother-in-law to be, at the time it was penned. Reading it now gives me an insight to emotions brimming on the edge of love and respect; something I would not have without the letter having been written on paper in pen. Some may not think this was a love letter but the romantic in me sees love, thus love letter.

This brings me to the heart of this piece, the love letter from God to His creation; stacked one atop the other and written by His mighty hand. The Bible, God's Word, His love penned by the prophets, disciples and apostles of Jesus, and inspired by the Holy Spirit. Each book of God's Word is a love letter written to each of us who read and chooses to believe. From creation to the triumphant return of Jesus, the Word is alive with God's plan, purpose and eternal love for His children. Much of the New Testament books are letters, written to encourage, admonish and witness to the recipients. We receive the love letters from God every time we open His Word and listen with open hearts and minds to what His voice is saying.

Love letters; a lost art? Maybe not, as I realize that the modern equivalent of email and texting can deliver the same message. Yet one simply cannot wrap up in red ribbon the text and emails and gain the same effect as the hand written letter. What has not changed through modern technology is God's Word. Whether you read His love letters with a leather bound bible in your hands or read from an app on your phone, His Word remains unchanged, the very same as it was first inspired to be.

# ONE HUNDRED

## Worship

John 4:23 "But the hour is coming, and is now here, when the true worshipers will worship the Father in spirit and truth, for the Father is seeking such people to worship him."

When do you worship God; Sunday morning, Wednesday night service, bible study? If we truly worship as we are intended to worship then we would worship continually. If we continually worship then every day would be Christmas, Valentine's, Easter and Thanksgiving. Intriguing, is it not? Take each event and break it down in the form of worship: Christmas, come let us worship Christ with us, Emanuel, Valentine's Day, love, worship the true God, who is love, Easter, worship the risen Christ, King of Kings, and finally, Thanksgiving, we worship with grateful hearts.

God is seeking us; He is calling you and me to worship Him as He is meant to be worshipped, in spirit and truth. The truth is that we absolutely have to feel the power of the worship. What power? The power of God with us. Zephanah 3:17 "The LORD your God is in your midst, a mighty one who will save; he will rejoice over you with gladness; he will quiet you by his love; he will exult over you with loud singing."

Every day is a day of worship. Every day becomes an event of celebration as we truly worship God as He not only deserves but intended from creation. We should worship in spirit and truth, worship God with us, God our Father who loves us, God our Savior who redeemed us, and God our provider in whom we owe everything and worship in gratitude. In this way we make every day a celebration of worship, worshipping the one true God, Emanuel, Love, Redeemer, Father...

# ONE HUNDRED-ONE

## The Old Oak Tree

Sitting underneath a six hundred year old oak tree...I plan on doing that one day soon now that I know there is one close by my home. Our Pastor dropped by for a visit last week and it was during our conversation that he told us about this oak tree and some of the town's history. It was fascinating as I have not learned much about Dublin; my husband and I both were raised in other places, only moving to the New River Valley in just the past few years. The promise of an afternoon of sitting in quiet contemplation underneath an ancient oak will have to wait though but I am so glad for the promise it holds for me. As for promises and trees they can readily be discovered in God's Word.

Psalms 52:8 "But I am like a green olive tree in the house of God. I trust in the steadfast love of God forever and ever." I am this verse, I live this promise. God has created in me a trust like no other of my life, as He has been here for me over and over again. Through trials, storms which brought fear and strife, through good times and blessings which brought peace and hope, God has been by my side during it all. He is faithful and although He did not need to earn my trust in His steadfast love, I have always known I could trust Him.

Isaiah 60:13 "The glory of Lebanon shall come to you, the cypress, the plane, and the pine, to beautify the place of my sanctuary, and I will make the place of my feet glorious." The sanctuary of the Lord is wherever I am as wherever I am He is with me. I imagine myself now under the six hundred year old oak tree and the glory of God surrounding me as I enter the sanctuary of His amazing grace.

God has promised great things to me and they begin with this;

Psalms 92:12 "The righteous flourish like the palm tree and grow like a cedar in Lebanon." Oh the promises of God and the power of revealing them through the strength of His creation, in this, the beauty of the tree.

Psalms 1:3 "He is like a tree planted by streams of water that yields its fruit in its season, and its leaf does not wither. In all that he does, he prospers." I will plant myself beneath that old oak tree and feel myself prosper in all the ways of the Lord as He has promised. The time of meditation, growing and evolving just as the leaves of that tree planted by the streams of water, will reaffirm my conviction and faith that my God is a mighty God and always fulfills His promises.

Made in the USA
Middletown, DE
15 May 2023

30613270R00078